Teaching Notes on Piano Exam Pieces 2005–2006

Grades 1–7

TIMOTHY BARRATT

JULIAN HELLABY

VANESSA LATARCHE

MARGARET MURRAY McLEOD

ANTHONY WILLIAMS

Teaching Notes on Piano Exam Pieces 2005–2006

Grades 1–7

With an introduction by CLARA TAYLOR, Chief Examiner of
The Associated Board of the Royal Schools of Music

The Associated Board of the Royal Schools of Music

First published in 2004 by
The Associated Board of the Royal Schools of Music (Publishing) Limited
24 Portland Place, London W1B 1LU, United Kingdom

© 2004 by The Associated Board of the Royal Schools of Music

ISBN 1 86096 417 6

AB 3008

Typeset by Hope Services (Abingdon) Ltd
Printed in England by Alden Group Limited, Oxford

CONTENTS

NOTES ON CONTRIBUTORS

Timothy Barratt, ARAM GRSM LRAM ARCM LMusTCL, is a professor at the Royal Academy of Music and Head of Keyboard at Dulwich College, London. He has toured extensively and broadcast as a solo pianist, accompanist and chamber music player. He adjudicates, directs workshops for teachers and is an Associated Board examiner, trainer, moderator and a mentor for the Board's Certificate of Teaching.

Julian Hellaby, MMus LRAM ARAM, studied piano at the Royal Academy of Music and subsequently performed throughout the UK and overseas. (His recordings of contemporary music include those broadcast recently by Australian national radio.) He is an Associated Board examiner, trainer and a mentor for the Board's Certificate of Teaching. He has extensive experience of piano teaching at all levels, and is currently Associate Senior Lecturer at Coventry University.

Vanessa Latarche, Hon ARAM FTCL LRAM ARCM, has established a reputation as a leading teacher. She is a professor at the Royal Academy of Music and an Associated Board moderator, trainer, examiner and presenter, working internationally in most capacities. As a performer she enjoys a busy concert schedule and gives broadcasts for the BBC. She is also an experienced adjudicator and gives masterclasses in the UK and abroad.

Margaret Murray McLeod, ARAM FTCL LRAM ARCM, studied piano and composition at the Royal Academy of Music. As well as performing as a soloist and accompanist, she has many years' experience of teaching at all levels. From 1972 she trained student teachers and performers at Napier University, Edinburgh, where she was Senior Lecturer for Performance Studies until 1997. Her work as a lecturer, examiner and adjudicator has taken her worldwide.

Anthony Williams, MMus Dip.RAM GRSM LRAM, has an active performing, teaching and adjudicating career in the UK and abroad and is currently Head of Keyboard and Instrumental Music at Radley College, Oxfordshire. He is an examiner (jazz and classical), trainer and moderator for the Associated Board as well as a mentor for its Certificate of Teaching. He is the co-author of previous *Teaching Notes*, with Clara Taylor, and the compiler of *Fingerprints* (Faber, 2002), a collection of original repertoire for piano teaching.

INTRODUCTION

Teachers always enjoy sharing professional insights. The contributors to these *Teaching Notes* – all distinguished teachers as well as being examiners – are no exception. Their enthusiasm shines out of the text and I know they have relished the detailed investigation into this exciting new syllabus. Writing commentaries is, of course, a very time-consuming exercise and regretfully it is no longer possible for me to be a regular contributor with the ever-increasing demands of the Associated Board's new initiatives. However, I am retaining a close interest and connection with these notes and take pleasure in providing the introduction.

The wide choice of repertoire for every grade gives the opportunity to match the pieces to the pupil. Sometimes you might choose a style that immediately suits, and at other times you might take a more medicinal approach in order to tackle shortcomings. From the lists there are obvious winners, which will appear many times in the exams, but do also explore the alternative pieces not published in the graded volumes. There are some delights to be found that may just be the answer for some pupils.

From Grade 1 to Grade 8 the three lists have more in common than you might expect. List A contains the technically demanding repertoire, List B the more warmly expressive pieces, and List C has a tremendous variety of styles, often with some jazzy rhythms. Despite the enormous difference in standards between Grade 1 and Grade 8, candidates' strengths and weaknesses tend to follow predictable paths in each list. I believe it will be helpful, therefore, to consider the three lists in more detail.

LIST A

In List A, definition of fingerwork, clarity of articulation and control of co-ordination are necessary, as fluency increases through the grades. These technical challenges, especially runs and ornaments, can upset the basic rhythm, and in their determination some candidates use an over-emphatic heavy touch that is self-defeating. An ability to keep the hands in exact ensemble is needed. Examiners often hear hands starting together then parting company at difficult corners. In higher grades, part-playing will often be a feature in List A and it's fairly rare to hear this successfully achieved. Many candidates over-emphasize the subject without adjusting the balance of the other lines. When this happens, control of dynamics and phrasing is inevitably affected.

Ornaments can be simplified or omitted in the early grades if they are causing problems with the rhythm. A steady basic beat is, of course, a higher priority than the decorations. In later grades some ornamentation is often necessary and certainly needs to be included to achieve higher marks.

In their efforts to manage the technicalities, many candidates are less aware of the musical content of the List A pieces. It's a delight to hear the right texture, clear dynamics and musical phrasing capturing the elegant style of the repertoire, which often comes from quite an early era.

LIST B

List B gives every opportunity to show more expressive phrasing and tonal warmth. The pieces are selected mostly from the Classical or Romantic styles, and cantabile tone will be needed for the melodies. Phrasing comes right to the forefront and balance of hands needs real care, as these pieces often follow the pattern of right-hand melody and left-hand accompaniment. Pedalling will be necessary for the more legato choices, with clean, rhythmic legato pedalling requiring good physical co-ordination. Even in higher grades we frequently hear the hands and the right foot not really coinciding.

Rubato is a vital part of musical phrasing and is often needed in the List B pieces. Candidates are usually better at slowing up than getting faster, so it will be helpful to explain the concept of a balanced rubato during the practice period.

Dynamics tend to be more smoothly graded in the styles chosen for this list, and ability to mould the tone evenly in each hand is something to aim for at all stages. Subtlety of tone colour and control of rubato within the stylistic discipline of the pieces are high priorities. Often the pieces have descriptive titles, giving a clue to the mood and atmosphere of the music.

LIST C

This list offers something for everyone. These days there is tremendous variety – jazz pieces, contemporary items and a host of other styles – which should make it easy to find exactly the right choice for your pupils.

In the early grades the jazz items are always hugely popular. Candidates can manage quite difficult rhythms when they like the music. Strongly rhythmic, dynamic pieces, such as the all-time hit *The Swinging Sioux* from the 1999–2000 Grade 1 syllabus, seem to capture the imagination of thousands of candidates throughout the world.

With such variety on offer, it's important to go to the heart of what each piece really requires to make an effective performance. Very often this means having a feel for the underlying beat, which will be more pronounced in the jazz pieces but still vital in many contemporary items. Colourful playing, evoking the various moods and sound worlds, will be enjoyable to explore, and candidates often feel they can relax and communicate these pieces, achieving more of a sense of performance than they manage with pieces from either to the two other lists.

Swung rhythm is an issue right from Grade 1. This is not the place to give a detailed description (which really needs a demonstration to make the point), but pupils will be helped imagining that 4/4 time becomes 12/8, so that a dotted quaver, semiquaver rhythm sounds more like crotchet, quaver. Pupils often catch on to this in certain parts of the piece, but find it difficult to be consistent, therefore causing the examiner to comment: 'Try to keep an even rhythm.' This does not mean that the swung rhythm has not been noticed, but usually indicates that there's an inconsistency in managing this throughout the performance. It is also perfectly acceptable to play the piece 'straight', especially in the lower grades, as long as the mood and relaxed feel of this style still come across. In the higher grades, the jazz pieces are quite sophisticated and often need a sense of swing and appreciation of whichever jazz style is appropriate to the piece.

In List C the metronome mark is often the composer's, so it pays to take notice and check carefully; as in Lists A and B, a metronome mark in square brackets indicates that it is an editorial suggestion, allowing a little more freedom of choice.

Young pupils often have a refreshingly open mind about contemporary items. Teachers may find some of the pieces slightly off-putting, but may be surprised to find that their students can get inside the music quite quickly and thoroughly enjoy playing in a different idiom.

Candidates are free to choose the order of their three pieces. It may well be wise to put the more technically demanding List A piece somewhere other than first in the exam. Many pupils these days start with their favourite piece, which helps confidence when they come to tackle the others. It is sometimes rather disappointingly obvious why a piece has been left until last!

The extensive selection for each grade should ensure that each one of your candidates is happy and comfortable with the choice and order of his or her pieces. As teachers will be well aware, the candidate's attitude of mind as he or she comes into the exam room is inevitably reflected in the result.

If you have any queries arising from this publication, do not hesitate to contact me, preferably by email (chiefexaminer@abrsm.ac.uk).

All good wishes to users of these notes, who will be inspired and reassured as the excellent selection of pieces becomes the graded pianistic diet for the coming exam sessions.

Clara Taylor

GRADE 1

Pupils will usually have been learning for up to eighteen months by the time Grade 1 is on the horizon. They may have taken the Prep Test during this time, in which case they will probably feel quite confident when facing this first real exam. A wide choice of pieces should help to keep motivation high, so why not have some alternatives prepared, then choose the best three as the exam approaches? The criteria for assessment for all grades are printed in *These Music Exams* – a useful source of reference for teachers.

A:1 S. Arnold *Giga*

'The giga is executed in a somewhat short and light fashion. Its character is for the most part one of cheerfulness…' So wrote an eighteenth-century commentator, and nothing much has changed in the intervening two hundred years!

The giga is a lively dance and this should come across in the character of your pupil's performance. Leaning into the downbeats, avoiding a feeling of six beats per bar, will help achieve this.

In the right hand, there is a considerable amount of moving around the keyboard. One way of practising the opening, to develop a sense of its geography, is to play all the right-hand notes in bar 1 together as a chord, then move the hand to the next bar, playing these notes as a chord, and so on. Once the moves are assured, the right hand needs a firm touch and a good legato with clear articulation – any overlapping will inevitably reduce clarity.

The editorial dynamics provide some welcome contrast and, if adopted, need to be clearly differentiated. Detaching the left-hand dotted crotchets a little will help to give the music a 'lift'. It is also stylish, since it was common practice in the eighteenth century to play such notes shorter than their written value. The quavers in bars 8 and 16 may be executed staccato.

A confident candidate may wish to start the exam with this piece. It gets the fingers moving and tests out the dynamic range of the piano – without requiring much subtlety at the opening!

A:2 Attwood *Andante*

This enchanting Andante is like a miniature aria, and singing the tune (an octave down) with your pupil can help reveal its cantabile nature.

The most natural places to 'breathe' are every four bars, and thinking this way will develop a sense of phrasing that transcends the bar lines. The piece needs to progress with a gentle motion, and the editorial metronome mark encourages this – too slow and you might run out of breath! A sensitive player might insert a *poco rit.* in bar 16 to ease in the reprise.

The trickiest aspect of this piece is probably the left-hand manoeuvres, which need to sound seamless. Practising descending triads of D minor/ A major/D minor then F major/C major/F major will be valuable in establishing the geography of these passages before adding the Alberti figuration. If the melody is to project, pupils will need to balance the hands, and for this it can be helpful to imagine that the right arm weighs more than the left.

The editorial dynamics require strong contrasts. The most interesting performances will also manage some rise and fall to enhance the phrase shapes. In the Sonatina, this Andante provides a moment of repose between two quite busy outer movements; it can also provide a moment of repose in the exam room.

A:3 Haydn *Tedesca*

This cheerful little number needs good humour in its delivery, so as to raise a smile. A good performance will, in addition, have a 'German Dance' feel. A sense of one in the bar, with just a hint of leaning into the downbeat, will help convey the necessary lilt.

It is appropriate to play the notes in the left-hand part detached. In fact, they could be detached throughout, providing buoyancy, but the more adventurous pupil may like to try the articulation suggested in bar 3 for all bars except those containing quavers. This would highlight the change in pattern at bars 9, 11 and 13. The busy left hand could easily weigh the texture down, but a mainly light touch allied to suitable articulation should keep it in the role of accompaniment.

The hands do not move about the keyboard much, the only real leaps occurring in the left hand around bars 8a and 16b. Here, pupils (once they are familiar with the notes) will benefit from looking at the keyboard while negotiating the jumps.

The level of dynamic is generally bold, although a softer echo might start at the end of bar 12, perhaps making a crescendo into the last bar. The pulse also needs to be sturdy, with no ritardando being necessary at any point.

A:4 Anon. *A Toy*

Playfulness is certainly part of this musical toy, and the suggested metronome speed reflects a sportive character. Crotchet = *c*.152 is quite fast, but not unduly so.

With the articulation as marked, the piece provides an excellent opportunity for contrasting legato and staccato touches, as well as supplying a musical setting for five-finger exercises – which can easily be practised outside this context! These phrases need to be even and flowing, and the pulse undisturbed by the small jumps around the keyboard such as those found in the left hand of bars 4–5 and 10–11. Observance of the staccato articulation, as a point of departure, will facilitate these manoeuvres as well as contribute to the music's character.

The character is light, almost dance-like, and a one-in-the-bar feel will help capture an appropriate style. The editorial dynamics serve as a useful guide, but it is as well to remember that the virginal – the instrument for which the piece was intended – was a delicate instrument. Over-forceful dynamics, even in the passage marked *forte*, could deprive the piece of its inherent playfulness.

The bright, cheerful character of this music may well appeal to the more extrovert of your pupils. The piece also provides a stimulus to explore older music and forerunners of the piano.

A:5 Martin Frey *Kleiner Kanon*

An attractively melodic composition, *Kleiner Kanon* has theoretical points of interest, too: apart from the obvious canon, both halves feature descending sequences. You might relate the piece to a round that your pupil knows, before explaining that here the imitation is not exact. (The first eight bars are a canon at the 7th; the rest, a canon at the 3rd.)

Genuine legato and evenness of touch are important. In the left hand, from bar 10 onwards, this can be aided by continuing to use the stronger fingers, fingering all quaver patterns with 4-3-2-4 – as long as your pupil plays the B♭s in bar 11 with the thumb, keeping the hand well forward. The material for both hands is equally melodic, so practising hands separately could seem musically rewarding; however, this should not be especially encouraged as appreciation of the overall interplay is crucial.

The dynamics need some thought. The left hand is marked with a stronger touch than the right, no doubt to counterbalance the right hand's natural ascendancy – rather than to imply that the right hand should be overshadowed by the left! Although no tempo indication is supplied, a gentle *moderato* will provide an appropriate pacing and allow for some desirable nuances within phrases.

A more able pupil might enjoy singing this as a duet with you – another valuable way of exploring musical possibilities.

A:6 Purcell *Air in D minor*

Elizabethan composers adopted the term 'air' to describe a vocal melody accompanied by other voices, or by an instrument. By the seventeenth century, in Purcell's time, the term was also used for solo keyboard music, although the melodic character remained.

An easy-going pace will bring out the melodic qualities and the suggested metronome speed seems to support this. It may be helpful to think of the first section, up to the double bar, in four-bar phrases – in which case the dynamics could be revised so as to lead up to and away from the first beat of the third bar within each phrase. The second section suggests a seamless eight-bar phrase, which the editorial dynamics will enhance. It is certainly helpful to think in phrases rather than bars.

Technically, the main challenge is one of mobility since neither hand stays in the same place for long; this is ideal for a pupil with a confident sense of keyboard geography. The piece also requires a sure legato, especially in the right hand where a very slight overlap from one note to the next (*legatissimo*) may be in order. A more able and adventurous candidate might like to experiment with a slightly detached (but definitely not staccato) left-hand accompaniment.

Overcoming the initial technical hurdles will be well worth the effort because the musical rewards are considerable. Friends and relations – as well as the examiner – will be entertained by this piece!

B:1 Grechaninov *March*

This forthright march should raise the spirits of even the most reticent candidate in a first exam. Imagining soldiers marching will help establish an appropriate tempo for the piece.

Character and strength will be achieved by a firm sense of rhythm, with care taken not to rush dotted crotchet/quaver patterns. The ends of lines might cause continuity problems, so looking ahead is essential for fluency.

The considerable repetition should aid learning (e.g. bars 5–8 = bars 17–20), and although some changes of position need practice, patterns generally fall comfortably under the fingers. A curved-finger position will help the intervals to be played exactly together (the right-hand interval of a 3rd in bar 9 needs particular care), and good finger independence is required for the semibreve in bar 3 to be held beneath cleanly articulated upper notes.

Making the unslurred crotchets detached will contrast with the smoother phrases, and despite the sparseness of dynamic indications, there is scope for imaginative shading within the *forte* level; bars 3–4, for instance, could be played less strongly than the opening. A really quiet *piano* echo at bar 13 is particularly effective. The choice of whether or not to slow down at the end should rest with your pupil – are the soldiers stopping or marching past?

B:2 Le Couppey *Arabian Air*

The minor key and flowing phrases present an opportunity for your pupils to play really expressively. The melody, which will be familiar to some players, could be sung initially (at an appropriate pitch), to develop a sense of the phrasing.

There are few changes of position in the right hand, but the left hand will need confident placing from bar 9 onwards, especially moving down to the dominant 7th in bars 15 and 23.

The tempo – not too brisk – should flow in crotchets; yet allow clarity and evenness to the semiquavers. The piece presents few rhythmic challenges, although care should be taken not to hurry rests at the ends of phrases.

The essentially legato line needs clear articulation in both hands; and good hand independence, in bar 9 and similar places, will maintain the smooth left-hand line while the right hand is lifted to repeat a note. Clearly defined phrasing, making gentle breaks at endings without 'bumping' the tone, will project the song-like character.

A sensitive candidate will allow the tone to rise and fall with the shape of each phrase. Using a stronger tone and emphasis will register the momentary change to the major at bars 9 and 17, and the sudden *forte* at bar 24 gives character and surprise before the very gentle ending.

B:3 Oesten *Das Echo*

Based on echoing phrases, this descriptive piece will appeal to imaginative pupils who enjoy exploring different registers of the piano.

The notes of the right hand are based on chord patterns played at different octaves. Care should be taken to move the hand in time, without disturbing the pulse, and while counting as full a minim as is possible. This may be your pupil's first encounter with triplets so it is important to 'feel' three regular beats in a bar. Clapping, or walking, the crotchets while you play the piece, then reversing roles, may help to establish the all-important reliable pulse.

Negotiating the dotted crotchet/quaver pattern in bars 15 and 17 needs attention to ensure that the note lengths are correct, the quavers not too short.

Practising the left-hand chords separately, listening for all notes sounding together, will help to establish patterns; using thumb and second finger for all 3rds (e.g. in bar 1) may prove the most reliable fingering.

A wide range of dynamics, with clear distinction between *forte* phrases and their echoes, will reflect the title and give character. Strong fingers are required for a firm *forte* tone, with the accents receiving special focus; isolated work on fourth and fifth fingers may be needed to develop this weaker part of the hand.

B:4 Brunner *Lesson in F*

The title gives little clue to the character of this charming song-like piece, which will suit sensitive, reflective pupils who enjoy a pleasing tune.

The tempo should reflect the *andante* indication, and while the notes in the first half fit mainly five-finger patterns, the second half contains more movement and intricacy, and should thus dictate the overall speed. The left-hand quavers from bar 9 will need careful practice with consistent fingering in order to preserve the rhythmic flow; it may prove beneficial to memorize the last two bars given the changes of position.

Singing the right-hand tune (shy pupils are often more willing to sing in duet with the teacher!), noticing where breaths are taken, will help establish how to create phrasing on the piano. Good legato is essential for clarity, checking in particular that the fourth and fifth fingers lift cleanly. In bars 1–2 and 5–6 the left hand should receive attention in order that the semibreves are held their full length beneath the moving line.

Inflections in dynamics will add musical interest, and contrasts should be clearly made (recording a pupil's performance can help clarify just how much is actually happening!). The final ritardando needs careful gauging to effect a gradual slowing-down.

B:5 Czerny *Study in D*

Most pianists play Czerny studies at some point in their training, and this is an especially tuneful introduction. The four phrases of the piece are all of equal length, and the right hand should 'sing' confidently over quieter left-hand broken chords.

At the start, the notes in the left hand seem easy, but careful practice will be needed to negotiate the changes of hand position from bar 7 onwards. Clean legato, with no overlap of the fingers, will ensure clear lines in the right hand, and the thumb should move under smoothly in bars 3 and 15. Synchronization of the hands (especially after tied notes, as in bar 2) may require attention.

Nervousness often causes candidates to rush, especially in the early grades, so practising setting an appropriate speed for each piece should form part of the preparation process. This piece should flow with two beats in a bar at an *allegretto* (not *allegro*) tempo; lightening the offbeat quavers, especially in the left hand, will help to achieve this.

The melodic line must be sensitively played in order to sustain interest. Most pupils will enjoy exploring (and writing in) extra dynamic detail. Locating the climax of each phrase, and of the piece as a whole, is a good starting point towards understanding this lyrical style.

B:6 Diabelli *Bagatelle in C*

The term 'bagatelle' means 'a trifle', and this characterful example should cheer any pupil preparing for a first exam.

The C major key and the almost total absence of accidentals mean that there are fewer hazards for the nervous candidate. In the final six bars of the left hand, however, there are changes of hand position which will require careful preparation. Practising the left hand in three-note chords will help the student learn the shapes confidently. Clear, nimble finger-work is necessary at this brisk, *vivace* pace, and the left hand's three-note slurs (with their implied break after the third note) can be interpreted loosely in the interests of preserving the one-in-a-bar impetus.

Keeping the left hand light, especially on second and third beats, will help to highlight the melody, which falls mainly into four-bar phrases (the final eight bars may be played as one phrase). Good co-ordination is also needed if the phrase endings in the right hand are to sound without disturbing the flow. Well-contrasted dynamics, shaping phrases according to their natural rise and fall, breathe musical life into the piece, and hence pupils should explore the *f–p* echo effects in the second half.

Whether a ritardando is needed at the end is a decision for your pupil – either way, the approach must be confident!

C:1 Brian Chapple *In the Pink*

A swinging and jaunty number, this will prove very popular. Examiners can anticipate, however, some very brisk performances, well over the speed limit, and in such cases, little charm or cheerfulness. There might also be unevenness, rushed rests and a few stumbles. Get the 'feel' and tempo right, though, and all will be well.

As far as the 'feel' is concerned, it is worth listening to some jazz pianists with your pupils, pointing out and imitating the way they play swung quavers. The slight accent on the shorter note is often very evident and adds real rhythmic push to the groove. In this piece, swung quavers might include the E in bar 3, the A♯ in bar 12 and the B♭ in bar 13. In such cases there should be a *subito piano* on the very next note – tricky to do but effective. Don't hesitate to bring in the right-hand G in bar 12 slightly before the bar line, with the left hand's E♭ remaining on the beat. This syncopation is absolutely in the nature of the piece.

The left hand is relatively straightforward, but precise rests will help the buoyancy – not forgetting that there is rhythm in the release of a note as well as in the playing of it.

In its simplicity and neatness of approach, and its colourful use of dynamics, this piece is suitable for virtually all young pupils.

C:2 Hovhaness *Sleeping Cat*

There is a captivating simplicity to this descriptive and dreamy piece. The gently lilting left hand perhaps contrasts the rise and fall of the cat's breathing, with the occasional sleepy stretch of its paws.

The first decision is to establish tempo, as anything too fast will destroy any sense of mood or picture. A steady crotchet beat will allow a more sensitive dynamic shape to the melody and aid control. Singing the melody or putting words to it will also help.

The left hand hardly moves from its original position, but do point out the note changes, especially to younger pupils (the change from D to C in bar 7 is one that might be missed). The accompaniment needs to be light and flowing, achieved by having the fingers close to the key surface at all times and by playing with a slightly 'pawing' feel on the surface of the key – nothing too direct or march-like.

The right hand must have character from the start, with the first D given slightly more emphasis than the following Bs. The minim should be particularly soft. In the third phrase encourage the pupil to listen to the quaver A which, after the dying-away C, should come in quietly and unaccented, the phrase then growing to the B of the next bar.

Bars 9 to 16, while not being too bright, could be at a louder dynamic; a change of colour here will enhance the piece. Each subsequent phrase may be gradually quieter, until the final velvety-pawed ending.

C:3 Timothy Jackson *Eeyore's March*

This is a fabulous, humorous piece with a great tempo marking. So many of Eeyore's miserable moments come to mind in the grumpy bass line, and if your pupil has never read any of the A. A. Milne books, then this could be some fun homework.

Technically, the piece is not without problems. Co-ordination between the hands is tricky at times, as is maintaining the right-hand staccato. That said, there are great musical rewards.

Begin by practising hands separately, not allowing a note together until both hands are fluent; in addition, lots of duet work will help train the ear and enable the phrasing to become second nature. This can be an opportunity to discuss tempo, articulation, balance and, importantly, the story behind the notes. A bounce at the wrist on to the end of the fingers will produce the right sound.

With hands together, playing legato may help the left hand in particular, which might otherwise play one note for each right-hand note in bars 4 and 8, for example. Once the hands can feel how they interact, that hurdle is passed.

Despite both hands being *forte* in the opening, the left hand should be to the fore throughout, holding some sound in reserve for the end. The left-hand melody should still be musically shaped within the dynamic level, however, with a little less on each subsequent E♭ in bar 3 and a crescendo through the quavers of bar 4.

Encourage the rudest of 'eey-ores' in bars 10–13, and the jokiest of endings, strictly in time and quiet.

C:4 Bartók *Children at Play*

Thirty seconds of sheer musical pleasure. Bartók does have a wonderful way with the piano miniature and the piece cries out 'personality' from the very start. As with the Paul Harris work in this C list, *Children at Play* develops the technique of playing couplets, demanding familiarity with the 'down/up' give in the wrist that ensures a controlled and short second note without tension.

Unlike the Harris piece, however, it is not necessary to achieve a softer staccato second note; there should be a little brightness achieved by a more active finger and a slight placing of the tenuto notes.

The added challenge is that the left hand has to provide a warm, legato backdrop to the sprightly, dancing melody of the opening. An over-legato, holding the bass notes with the finger and keeping the weight towards the outside of the hand, will avoid an interrupting thumb. This will help prevent the character-destroying mechanical articulation often heard in Alberti-style bass accompaniments.

Some musical features will greatly enhance the piece's personality. Most significant must be applying dynamics and shaping the phrases, starting with the markings already given. As always, insist on the decrescendos being very obvious; recording a pupil's performance really does show how much variety is needed to make the piece effective.

Do use the suggested fingering, which works well. Ensure that all the rests are observed and encourage a controlled ritenuto at the end, the piece almost finishing mid-sentence.

C:5 Janina Garścia *The Goldfishes*

A goldfish has only a few seconds' memory, and the idea that the goldfish bowl is a new experience each time around is a fascinating one. While this probably didn't enter the composer's mind, the repeat of the opening in bar 9 could well be a second circuit of the bowl. If so, a fresh musical perspective would be a bonus.

There are no major technical demands in this attractive, relatively straightforward piece. The main challenge will be the treble clefs of the opening, particularly for those who connect the treble clef with the right hand rather than understanding its indication that all notes are above middle C. Familiarization with this in a lesson may pay dividends.

Otherwise, it is a matter of giving the melody musical shape, particularly at the ends of phrases, which will need a light final note (bars 4, 8 and so on).

A little easing of the tempo at the first double bars will help introduce the middle section's bolder tone and dynamic level. Follow this with another slight ritardando into the repeat of the opening and, at the end, a soft, final A.

For teachers who integrate aural skills into the teaching of a piece there is plenty of scope here. Teaching phrases by ear and then encouraging pupils to work out fingering, for example, and playing 'spot the mistake' will all help listening skills, memory and, above all, bring out the musical possibilities. As with all pieces which are not too troublesome, demand musical finesse and polish, using this opportunity to 'fish' for hidden musical depths!

C:6 Paul Harris *Springboard*

Aptly titled, this is a lively and jolly piece which, with its jaunty three-in-a-bar and tuneful melody, disguises a slightly tricky study in couplet phrasing and offbeat rhythms. To this end it will be necessary to focus on the all-important 'give' in the wrist, while reinforcing the musical context within which this is being practised.

The couplets should be played with no rigidity, the wrist dropping for the first of the pair as the arm descends and then rising in a 'down-up' gesture to allow a softer and relaxed lift. As pliancy in the wrist is so much the key to future success, and will help avoid tension aches and pains, it is really worth taking the time to get this right. In bars 5 and 6 the hands rise and fall together, with a higher, relaxed wrist for the upbeats, the gesture itself enabling the dynamic phrasing.

Shades of dynamics are all-important; the first small phrase (bars 1–2) might be shaped towards the D, and the second (with no accent on the first note) could make a crescendo towards the C. Bars 5 to 8 might start *piano* and grow in level towards the first beat of bar 7, before dying away.

Bars 13 to 16 are tricky. Many will focus so much on the hemiola that the left-hand change of chord may go unnoticed. Point this out, together with details of articulation and rhythm, and notice the tied note of the final section ending with a staccato dot – an indication to release immediately the bass note is played.

GRADE 2

Lessons will have been learnt from Grade 1, and pupils will probably want to play something similar to their favourite piece from the last exam. The pacing of the preparation, not forgetting the supporting tests, will probably be easier with the experience of Grade 1 safely in the past.

A:1 Anon. *Musette*

Many pupils enjoy the strong rhythm and athleticism of this familiar favourite. The leaps may prove challenging to some pupils, so glancing quickly between music and keyboard will be necessary at times.

The piece is in ternary form, with the da capo forming the third section of the ABA structure. Firm fingers are needed to give the semiquavers clarity, and care should be taken to synchronize the hands exactly in bars 1–2. Arriving accurately and on time for the F♯s in bar 3 requires both courage and precision; 'spotting' both notes in advance will help. Confident main beats with lighter subsidiary notes will give character to the rhythm, and there is scope for varying the dynamic levels every two bars, perhaps using a quieter tone in bars 3–4 and 7–8.

There are more potential pitfalls in bars 9–20, so establishing confident fingering and both thinking and looking ahead are essential. Moving the left-hand position in bar 12 may need isolated practice, especially for a small hand. Bars 13–16 have an almost jazzy feel. The marked phrasing highlights this, but so can detaching the unslurred quavers. The dynamics overall should be well contrasted.

Anxious candidates often hurry, especially in music with its own momentum. A firm sense of pulse and forthright phrasing will help ensure a poised, stylish performance.

A:2 Purcell *Rigadoon*

This jaunty dance in the welcome key of C major is a good piece for introducing part-playing in the left hand.

The notes on the page look easy, but an octave stretch is needed to do justice to the left hand. Organized fingering is needed throughout, and the second half must have considerable practice before there is ease with the held notes and shifts of left-hand position (especially in bars 10–12). It is not always possible to join notes, particularly when the thumb moves position, but minims should be held for as long as possible. Dividing the left-hand part between the two hands is a good practice method for sorting out and listening to the parts.

The right hand poses few problems apart from fitting in the ornaments, and initial practice without them will establish the framework into which they fit. For the trills, care is needed to pace the triplet quavers evenly (semiquavers, though more notes, may be the easier option rhythmically).

The two-in-a-bar time signature will give sprightliness to the rhythm – if offbeat notes are played lightly. This vitality can be further enhanced by detaching unslurred crotchets, thus marking the contrast with the slurs. In addition to the editorial dynamics, greater tonal variety within each half is possible; for example, dropping back in tone at bar 12 before making a crescendo towards the end.

A:3 Telemann *Minuetto*

Grace and charm are two words which readily come to mind in this dance by Bach's one-time rival, Telemann. Despite the one-in-the-bar feel, the tempo must be spacious and unhurried to capture the idiom (as reinforced by the given metronome mark).

The right hand has the main melodic interest throughout, accompanied by a left hand which leaps around the keyboard. There are few accidentals to worry about, and detaching the unslurred quavers negates the need for a large stretch. If an alternative fingering for the left hand of bar 16 is wanted, consider 5-1-4-3-2.

When tackling ornaments, consider first practising without them to establish a firm pulse. If adding them proves problematic, you could simplify the realizations – playing the right hand of bar 8, for example, as a semiquaver triplet followed by a crotchet to coincide with the left hand.

Dance-like buoyancy will come about if the second and third beats are generally lightened. Slurs need care in order to avoid accenting the second note. The remaining quavers, meanwhile, can be detached or not (for instance, the right-hand quaver in bar 1 could be slurred), depending on the taste and skill of the performer.

A:4 J. F. F. Burgmüller *Arabesque*

This delightful piece, which combines finger agility in both hands with strong musical character, is a real 'winner' with most pupils.

Although the chosen tempo should reflect the *allegro scherzando* indication, starting too fast invariably results in problems when the left hand plays semiquavers in bars 11–16. A reliable pulse is crucial for success, resisting the temptation to rush at crescendos, and fingerwork is going to need clarity and evenness. A light arm will allow the hand to 'travel' to the next position (especially important for the final six bars), and care should be taken not to 'bump' the final quaver of each semiquaver group. Bars 17–18 and 30–31 are potential danger spots worthy of special practice, as are the repeat bars (for the exam, repeats are not required, however).

Lightly detached left-hand chords, with all notes sounding (the fifth finger often fails to 'speak'), will establish rhythmic impetus at the outset. The dynamics, meanwhile, should be well contrasted. Notable features include the second-beat accent in bar 8 and the sudden drop to *piano* at bar 23. Exploring long legato lines in the right hand of bars 11–18 will give good contrast with the detached outer sections.

Finally, a ritardando in bar 30 will allow time to place the final chord, which should sound confident and triumphant.

A:5 Graupner *Air en Gavotte in C*

Neatness and agility are two qualities which readily spring to mind for this 'piece in the style of a Gavotte'. The *Air* was probably written for the harpsichord and the instrument's precise 'attack', and it contains the characteristic rhythmic feature of starting each phrase at the half-bar.

Close printing makes the piece appear complex, but the quavers lie mainly in scale patterns. However, the middle section, starting after the first repeat sign, will probably require more practice than the outer sections (the da capo should be played), and care should be taken to synchronize the hands exactly, not losing rhythmic impetus when fitting in the occasional quavers in the left hand. Initial left-hand practice omitting the staccato will give confidence in moving around the keyboard. Note that the 'wedge' signs simply indicate ends of phrases and should not disturb the flow.

'Thinking' towards the first beat of the bar, with light upbeats, gives impetus and poise to the rhythm (at an *allegretto* tempo), and dynamic contrasts between phrases need clarity and confidence, especially the *piano* 'echo' near the end.

Negotiating the suggested phrasing, which requires good hand independence and an agile quaver staccato, may prove problematic to some pupils. If so, staccato crotchets and legato quavers throughout would be a good alternative.

A:6 Haydn *Minuet in G*

'Minuet' must be one of the most popular titles for an exam piece, but the style of this graceful dance does not come easily to some pupils of the twenty-first century. Providing a picture, real or imaginary, of elegantly dressed eighteenth-century dancers with unhurried movements might help promote the right mood. Setting a suitable tempo to reflect this idea is crucial, and the rhythmic characteristic of a third-beat start to each phrase needs to be 'felt' by thinking towards the next bar, with lightened second beats, especially on the repeated thumb notes.

The right-hand notes generally fall comfortably under the hand, although the fingering in bars 7 and 8 may need modifying for a small stretch. Memorizing the 'corner' at bars 13–14 will increase the likelihood of an accurate jump if the span cannot be reached. The left hand hops around the keyboard, but noticing common notes between successive chords, for example the middle C in bars 2 and 3, will give confidence and security.

Playing one hand quieter than the other poses difficulties for many young players. In this instance, however, lightly detached left-hand chords will help to highlight the melodic line. Over the main dynamic levels the sensitive candidate will shape the quavers to bring this charming music to life.

B:1 Gedike *Barcarolle*

Artistic students who enjoy dreamy pieces will play this barcarolle well. The right hand here imitates the singing of the Venetian gondolier, and the left hand's lilting rhythm represents the rocking of the boat. The successful performer will have an ability to maintain control over the flowing pulse and a good legato.

The melody line sits neatly under the hand, requiring a smooth singing sound for the four-bar phrases (the last phrase, however, extends to five bars). At this level, candidates often have difficulty in thinking in long phrases, and seeing the slurs in each bar can mislead, causing phrasing to be in short units and giving a bar-by-bar feel. Encourage your students to feel musical sentences of four bars by singing along with them. Putting words to the melody will find the natural points of emphasis in the phrase.

The left hand needs a light thumb, but the quavers at the ends of bars should not be cut too short or accented, but gently lifted to give the desired floating effect.

The dynamics are clearly marked, with undulations of crescendos and diminuendos. These should not become overblown, though; suggest to your pupil that the level reaches *mezzo-forte* at most in the middle of them. Bars 11 and 12 could be played as a *pianissimo* echo for extra colour. The last phrase presents a change of register reaching up high – the romantic gondola disappearing around the bend of a tranquil canal.

B:2 Maikapar *The Moth*

What child could fail to be entranced by such an imaginative piece as this? It is beautifully written at the top of the piano, and the leger-line reading, at first, will take some organization. Both hands are written in the treble clef, and the lowest note of the left hand is A above middle C. Candidates may wish to move the piano stool to the right so as to have the notes in front of them. This is dangerous and should not be recommended, particularly as they may forget to readjust the position for their next piece when under pressure. Most children should be able to reach, slightly leaning their body to the right.

The piece needs a delicate touch, and its dynamics are contained within a limited range, not reaching more than *mezzo-piano*, say, at bar 11. Pupils may drop the hand on the semiquaver patterns in the right hand. This promotes physical freedom, but guard against too much of an accent on the drop. Encourage them to think over the bar line, on to the first beat of the bar.

The tempo must be lively for the insect to take flight and to achieve the *volante* marking. The *poco rit.* at the end needs careful timing, the rests needing their full value. The semiquavers in bar 19 are back in tempo, just before another ritardando, when the last flutter of gossamer wings takes the moth to its resting-place.

B:3 Schubert *Deutscher No. 2*

A German dance of the Ländler variety (written by Schubert at nineteen years old), it is quite quick, with a feel of one-in-a-bar. As such it demands a deft left hand. Indeed, the fingering, stretches and jumps in the bass make the piece more suited to larger hands, to the older child or adult.

As ever with pieces of melody and accompaniment, the balance of the hands is extremely important. Chords in the left hand must not overpower the right-hand melody, which needs to be played with a good cantabile quality throughout. There is a strong feeling of lilt which can be achieved by ensuring that the first beats of each bar in the left hand are more prominent than the second and third beats – chords which should be lifted in style. From bar 9 the dotted minims in the bass line should be held if possible, though examiners will understand if the candidate cannot stretch. The right-hand melody would benefit from lightly detaching the first and second notes in bars 1, 3 and 5.

In the second section, the acciaccaturas may present problems to the inexperienced player. If so, it will help to begin by playing the grace note together with the note it precedes, gradually separating the two notes later. Often, players will accent the grace note and play it too slowly and heavily, weighing down the texture.

This is a charming waltzing dance, but it should be matched to the pupil with care.

B:4 Enckhausen *Allegretto in A*

If your pupils can make a pleasing cantabile sound, then this is the piece for them. Good quality of tone, a singing right hand and well-judged balance between the hands will be necessary in order to portray the charm of this music. Its attractive melody will prove popular with performers and listeners alike.

At first, counting the piece in six is useful for correct rhythm, but the ultimate aim is to feel it in two, to capture the lilting style. The suggested metronome mark (dotted crotchet = 92) seems about right for this piece.

Lots of practice of A and E major scales should ensure smooth playing of the right hand. For consistency of fingering in this hand, you might suggest that bars 14 to the end are given the same patterns as in bars 6–8, namely finger 3 on C♯ (instead of 2) and 2-3-1-2-3-4-5 to finish the pattern. The fingering of repeated notes is always a matter for debate, but as long as the eventual sound is musical, how it is achieved is incidental. If your students, therefore, find the left hand in bars 5, 6, 13 and 14 easier to control with repeated thumbs, then do change the suggested 2-1 fingering. Small hands will find the stretch from fingers 5 to 2 in bars 5 and 13 rather difficult anyway.

All in all, the performance will be successful if the tone is well controlled, with smooth grading of legato crescendos, the climax being reached in the middle of the piece.

B:5 Kabalevsky *Waltz in D minor*

Choosing repertoire to suit a pupil's particular character and abilities is one of the skills of good teaching, and this delightful dance will appeal to the child with an artistic bent. The key features for success are good control of the dynamics and independent articulation between hands.

Crisp chord-playing in the left hand (which is marked *sempre staccato*) is needed to maintain rhythmic buoyancy. However, the right hand needs a well-produced legato touch to enhance the elegance of the melody. Much separate-hand practice should be encouraged, not only at the beginning of the learning process but also as a regular routine in order to develop the musical shaping. It may be difficult for small hands to stretch the octaves in, for example, bar 3, so well-negotiated jumping will be necessary, though try to avoid clipping the lower A as the hand leaps.

In this expressive piece, the dynamic range is from *piano* to *mezzo-forte* only, so any attempt to overproject the sound will destroy the light style, making it rather leaden and heavy-footed. The *pochiss rit.* in bar 16 must be enough to make its point, rather than impede the musical progress. Towards the end, the diminuendo takes the dancers twirling away into the distance on their toes, concluding with a graceful curtsey in the final two bars.

B:6 M. Vogel *Moderato in C*

This flowing piece demands control in the fingers so as to maintain a feeling of *moderato* without any sense of rushing forward. The examiner will be pleased to hear evenness of touch and an ability to hold the tempo. Since pianists are not required to breathe to make a sound on their instrument, they often overlook this vital 'punctuation' in the phrasing. Encouraging pupils physically to breathe, however, will help younger players in particular to keep control throughout.

There is opportunity for a wide range of dynamic interest here. The hair-pins (often children are not familiar with this rather old-fashioned term!) should not be overblown, reaching *mezzo-forte* at the tops of phrases as in bar 3 and bar 12. However, the *forte* in bars 7 and 17 should be sudden, but always *dolce* in quality. Gauging the weight of the accents on the minim chords in bars 6 and 16 will take extra care, too. It may be advisable to treat these as tenuto markings, since they occur at the end of a diminuendo. Practice in covering the chord shapes under the hand will help to control the chords in the diminuendo.

With a sense of line in the left-hand crotchets (especially in the second half), the piece eases down with a final diminuendo. Careful placing of the final chords should bring the music to its resting-place.

C:1 Absil *Musette*

When we think of a musette, we normally imagine something quite cheer-ful but here is one that is rather doleful and subdued. It also provides a primer in changing meters.

One way of introducing the alternating time-signatures is to count the bars out loud in a teacher–pupil exchange and, once this is established, to clap the actual rhythms. Although the pace is quite slow, the pulse needs to be regular with only one ritardando at the end. However, the right-hand semiquaver passages in particular need some flexibility.

The left-hand chords sound better if played undetached. It will be help-ful for pupils to practise keeping the hand in contact with the keys, just lift-ing sufficiently to ensure that the chord is repeated and, maybe, pedalling the bars containing quavers. A certain monotony in this part is entirely appropriate, all the melodic interest being taken by the right hand. The dynamic is mostly subdued so, if the piece is not to be unduly mono-chrome, the indicated hairpin nuances must be heard. Obviously, the *sforzandi* need to stand out – although not percussively – and pedal may be employed both to aid the effect and to connect the note with the next bar. Pedal can also be used to join the C♯ of bar 22 to the subsequent chord; the *una corda* pedal could enhance the last bar.

The more inward-looking pupil will enjoy this piece, and examiners will appreciate performances which capture its pathos through a sensitive approach.

C:2 Colin Matthews *Rosamund's March*

This piece is great fun once the 'extended technique' aspect has been taken on board. It will appeal to those extrovert pupils who like to shed inhibitions at the piano!

The obvious feature to master is the fist clusters which – the composer advises – need not be absolutely precise. However, it is a good idea to find the top note so that the melody's triadic and scalic nature is not lost. A free-fall forearm drop into the cluster from about two inches (5 cm) above the keyboard will achieve the necessary *forte* dynamic, gradually rising to about four inches above for the concluding *fortissimo*. Although the left hand is marked *piano sempre*, it must be loud enough for notes not to be lost under the pelting from the right hand!

The pace is steady, creating a sense of mock pomposity, but the pulse must be regular, remaining stable when the right hand moves from the downbeat to the offbeat at bar 4 and in reverse, at bar 27. The middle section can be more flexible, as the military burlesque is abandoned and the mood becomes 'thoughtful'. The composer permits pedal here but perhaps it is not necessary – all the articulation can be achieved by good fingering.

This piece could be a good antidote to nervous tension in the exam room. For further examples of this style of music, listen to pieces by Henry Cowell.

C:3 Christopher Norton *Get in Step*

Here is a blues march, the first of two pieces in this list that use the C blues scale. Whereas *Timewarp* is all mystery, however, this needs military precision.

It should be felt as a brisk two in the bar and any tempo much below the suggested marking will probably sound too effete. It should be dry throughout, the staccatos employing fingertip crispness but with active lower finger-joints to avoid too delicate a dynamic. This will also highlight the first note of the slurs. Some useful groundwork here may be to practise a scale in slurred couplets alternating with staccato pairs.

Technically, there are no real problems, though pupils will have to get used to playing with their hands three or more octaves apart. The marked fingering is helpful (especially for smaller hands), but, if you want to economize on thumb use, you could adopt 5-4-3-2-1-3-2-1 for the opening left-hand pattern.

The dynamics need to be strongly projected, but room should be left for the central crescendo. There is no call for rubato and, in fact, this piece can benefit from practising to a metronome since stability of pulse is crucial. The syncopation of the final bar could surprise your pupil – this little bit of out-of-step mischief suggests that we don't need to take the march too seriously after all.

C:4 Peter Gritton *Timewarp*

Both title and music strongly suggest some kind of story. A lot happens in a brief span and, as the right and left hands climb out in opposite directions, a climactic event is anticipated. Although based on the 12-bar blues, this piece perhaps gives pride of place to creating an atmosphere. However, it does provide an ideal opportunity to explore also the C and G blues scales.

Maybe your story will concern entering a type of sci-fi timewarp; certainly musical 'timewarps' can be found in the rhythm. Much of the right-hand phrasing emphasizes 3/4, and clear observation of marked accents will project this feature. Most pupils will have little difficulty in 'warping' the right-hand quavers into threes in the 9/8 bar but they may experience problems reverting to 4/4. Here, careful counting in quavers will help overcome any tendency to distort the rhythm.

Fingering this piece is mainly straightforward, though you might consider using 4-3-2-1 in beats 3 and 4 of bars 9 and 10, as this matches right-hand position to melodic shape. Left-hand staccato crotchets need to be kept light to maintain the balance.

Playing the music at a moderate pace (crotchet = *c*.112 is really quite steady) will help create atmosphere, as a hasty reading cannot generate mystery. Attention to dynamics is crucial: the piece presents a wonderful exercise in crescendo control and the *fortissimo* at bar 9 – if graded successfully from a *piano* opening – will be exciting for both candidate and examiner.

C:5 Lajos Papp *Rhythm Playing*

Those of you who use Bartók's *Mikrokosmos* will be familiar with the Bulgarian-style dance rhythm which this piece adopts. At the same time, this piece has the character of a study in alternate-hand playing.

The actual notes are straightforward enough and all lie within a three-octave range. The main challenge to the fingers is in producing a sharp, percussive staccato as well as a good contrasting legato. Rhythmic precision is of the essence, and clapping games with your pupil to instil a sense of 'two plus three' could be useful preparation for overcoming the desire to round the bar lengths up or down.

The character is boisterous, favouring a predominantly loud dynamic, and the *forte* passages call for quite an aggressive attack, projecting the staccato notes with shard-like pointedness. However, a significant drop is needed for the *mezzo-forte* phrases, where the accents must convey the all-important rhythmic construction. While the tempo should be a genuine *allegro*, if the pace is too fast some of the spirit could be lost – a controlled momentum is more exciting than frenzy!

The more extrovert of your pupils should enjoy this piece, and a successful performance will bring an explosion of vitality into the exam room – possibly making for a rousing conclusion to the performance of the pieces.

C:6 Prokofiev *The Cat*

Lovers of the orchestral original will enjoy having the chance to play this piano arrangement, by Carol Barratt. With the feline furtiveness preserved, pupils might relate this to images of their own domestic puss.

The right-hand part calls for a light, fingertip staccato over a delicate but 'well-sprung' left-hand accompaniment (cats should never seem leaden-footed!). The offbeat slurred couplets (bars 7 and 18) may seem a little unnerving at first, but a 'drop-lift' sensation in the wrist and forearm should achieve the required accentuation. This technique can usefully be practised within G and C major scales, too. However, accents must not be too harsh if pantomime is to be avoided!

Pupils with a decent span may like to try the G major chord in bar 8 with finger 2 on the lowest note, and then the C/D of bar 9 with the thumb. Likewise, bar 15 can be accommodated by using the thumb on middle C before 5/2 on the ensuing 6th.

A regular pulse (at *moderato*) is necessary, but there should be a feeling of suppleness, too – cats do not march in military fashion! A sense of two- rather than four-in-the-bar may aid this. Note the overall increase in dynamics, and that too quiet a start will make the drop to *pianissimo* in bar 8 unattainable. The last four bars bring the piece to a bold conclusion, demonstrating that it is possible to end outside the original key.

GRADE 3

Perhaps it is time to be a little more adventurous in the choice of pieces, now that exams are quite a familiar experience. Something of quite a different style might broaden the pupil's outlook, so do explore the alternative pieces as well as the printed selection.

A:1 Dieupart *Passepied*

That this dance was written for the harpsichord gives the teacher the opportunity to explain the instrument and demonstrate the lightness of touch needed to imitate the timbre. Children will not have had much exposure, if any, to this early keyboard instrument, so playing harpsichord recordings to them will open their ears to the particular sound of the instrument, and the musical style of this period. Better still, if you have access to a harpsichord, let your pupils try their piece out on it. This will create much excitement, and it is amazing what can be absorbed just from exposure to the unfamiliar sound and touch.

This Baroque dance looks fairly simple on the page but it is, in fact, quite challenging. The part-playing in the left hand requires careful attention. In bars 1–8, for example, the notes on the first *and* second beats are held throughout the bar, while bars 12–15 will need extra practice to ensure accuracy. Playing the left hand's two parts with both hands will allow your pupils to hear what they are aiming for. The twirling right-hand quavers need to be even, and shaped, throughout. Most patterns lie well under the hand, although bars 12–14, again, will need detailed attention.

The editorial slurring implies a legato touch for the melody line. Care must be taken, however, not to clip the ends of slurs at the end of each bar, otherwise the longer four-bar phrases will sound disjointed.

This piece will not suit everyone, but those who succeed in mastering it will have acquired very useful skills in part-playing and for tackling Baroque pieces in the future.

A:2 Rathgeber *Aria*

The key of A major and the compound quadruple time give this Aria a cheerful character, which, if played at the suggested tempo and with some musical shape in the line, will bring a smile to the faces of both player and listener.

Note that the printed dynamics and slurring are editorial. Should a candidate play a different scheme of dynamics, the examiner will respect this and not penalize the change, as long as the result is musically coherent and within the boundaries of style and good taste. Note that there are possibilities, also, for adding extra echo phrases, in bars 5 and 12.

The right-hand quavers must be evenly played, with a rise and fall in the shaping. Particular care is needed with the repeated As in bar 1, similarly the Es in bar 7. A slight stress on the first quaver of each group and a lighter attack on the third quaver will provide buoyancy, while feeling towards the third beat in the bar will help overall shaping. In bar 2 (similarly bar 8) allow the dynamic to follow the contours of the line, rising up to D and down to the close of the phrase on the third beat A, though care must be taken to avoid an exaggerated swell in the line. The left-hand chords need not be smoothly connected. A non-legato touch, with tiny gaps between chords, is appropriate for this style, though one chord-shape should be held for as long as possible before moving to the next. Playing the chords staccato must be avoided, since this will destroy the lyrical element of the Aria.

At the end of the piece, a relaxing of the tempo over the last bar will give a sense of finality.

A:3 S. Wesley *Sonatina in B flat*

This attractive keyboard piece will charm both performer and listener. It is pianistic and, with its articulation and dynamics well executed, it will provide a sunny opening to any candidate's exam programme.

The piece has a ternary ABA form, so from the outset it would be prudent to explain this, showing that the last section is an exact repeat of the first. This, in effect, gives only 16 bars of actual note learning.

Examiners often hear well-prepared openings of pieces, and are saddened to hear middle sections fall down, since these are often more difficult and yet may not have had as much time spent on them in the learning process. We all recognize the child who likes to play the beginning at breakneck speed, before realizing that the middle cannot be achieved at that pace. It would therefore be a good investment to bracket bars 9 to 16 and suggest that these are tackled first in the practice regime – even before the opening is played. These bars demand independence of the fingers and are imitative, co-ordination of the hands being the biggest challenge. It will help pupils to play the right hand while you play the left, and vice versa, so that they can become accustomed to hearing the two parts. Eventually they can build the section up in two-bar segments (stopping at the end of each two bars), then play in four bars, and so on; in this way the section can be built rather like a jigsaw puzzle.

This little Sonatina would make a splendid choice for school concerts, as its melody is very appealing.

A:4 C. P. E. Bach *March in D*

It is reassuring to see in the A list this familiar piece (by one of J. S. Bach's sons), which, as part of the Anna Magdalena Bach Book, is part of the staple diet for young players. This lively march should be felt in two (*alla breve*), not a slow four. Demonstrations of marching around the room can encourage your student to feel the two beats, in addition to providing entertainment for you both.

An inventive approach to dynamics is needed here. The possibilities include a crescendo to the end of bar 9 and again towards bar 22, otherwise a diminuendo into bar 13 and a crescendo up to the top of the melodic line (bar 16), to drop down again in bar 17.

The weight and length of the left-hand crotchets need careful consideration. It is always interesting to hear authentic performances on CD, and listening to Baroque pieces with basso continuo in particular will encourage your pupil to imitate that sound. Inevitably, the right-hand thumb will play the minims in bars 1, 2, 10 and 11. Make sure these are not too heavy.

The trill in bar 7 will, naturally, cause anxiety, and so incorporate this into the practice regime from an early stage. A triplet starting on the C♯ – as indicated by the appoggiatura (C♯, B, C♯) – and then two quavers (B and the last A in the bar) would work well here.

Overall, a sprightly feel and detached first beats in the right hand in bars 1, 2, 4, 5, 10, 11, 13 and 17, will give this march a spring in its step. Pupils with an ability to play with good clarity of touch will enjoy this piece.

A:5 Mozart *Allegro in B flat*

Written in Salzburg, and when Mozart was just six years old, this Allegro could be introduced to your students as a 'conversation piece', with its myriad musical questions and answers. There are plenty of opportunities for making creative echo phrases in this delightful piece; indeed, repetitions of the same material (in bars 3, 5 and so on) must have contrast. Highlighting the sequence in bars 17 to 20 by playing more quietly than in the previous four bars will also add interest.

Timing in this piece is the key for good control. Nervousness during the exam can cause rests to be overlooked, especially by the young performer. The quaver rests in this piece must be given their full value. Similarly, the crotchet chords on the first beats of bars 4, 6 and so on are to be held fully, yet played with slight emphasis as they are at the ends of phrases.

The acciaccaturas should be incorporated gracefully with light fingers, to give a 'snap' to the melodic line. The printed slurs give the piece buoyancy, though this slurring should be thought of more as bowing a string and be gently lifted, not too clipped.

The closing bars could be played loudly or quietly. It may be a good idea to play both ways to your pupil and decide together which is best. Whatever your choice, the last chord needs placing, with a little time taken over the last bar line.

A:6 Pleyel *Menuetto in C*

In this sophisticated Parisian dance one can readily conjure up images of an eighteenth-century ballroom: ladies in beautiful gowns and dancers moving gracefully through their steps. This imagery helps to pinpoint an appropriate tempo for the piece, and musically shaping the dynamics – with crescendos and diminuendos, as suggested – will help convey the general elegance of the style.

From the outset, the repeated chords need careful gradation to communicate the poise inherent in this style. This can be achieved by thinking through the chords and on to the first beat of the phrase's second bar, giving the piece the musical lilt that it needs.

Although the written quavers of the Trio (in F major) suggest a more flowing feel, the pace must not quicken with the increased finger activity. Here, after the broader statements of the menuet, the two-bar phrases create a sense of question and answer. Guard against overdoing the accents in bars 21 and 22 – especially since the dynamic will be raised up to a *mezzo-forte* from the crescendo in bar 20 – and always keep the tone sweet. Remember, too, that examiners expect to hear the da capo. On the second time round, at the very end of the menuet, it would be appropriate to slow down slightly, giving a feeling of finality.

B:1 Gurlitt *Song*

There is a graceful lilt to this song that suggests the swaying movements of a waltz. Of course the right-hand melody must sing, even when it is marked *piano*, but it is the left hand that supplies the rhythmic impulse to the music. The jumps in this hand will require special attention so that they become fluent and safe. Encourage the use of either third or fourth finger on the lowest notes of the second-beat chords, reserving the fifth finger for the first-beat bass notes and the dominant 7th chord in bar 30. Above all, keep the left hand light and buoyant.

Accents on the second half of second beats should be avoided, especially in the middle section where both hands play quavers together (there is a danger of it swinging into compound duple time), and when practising the right hand alone, your pupil should feel the quaver groups moving towards the first beat of the next bar. Soon both hands will be dancing along happily with a one-in-a-bar pulse.

The suggested pedalling will give an extra lift to the accompaniment of the principal theme and help to highlight the bass notes, too. At bar 17 the use of legato pedalling, changing on the first beat of each bar, will add fullness to the texture and help to build the excitement of the *poco animato* towards the climax in bar 23. However, providing the longer notes (such as in bars 6–8) are fully sustained, it is possible to create a satisfying and musical performance of this charming piece without any pedal at all. At Grade 3 some players are not yet ready or even tall enough to use the pedal confidently.

B:2 Tchaikovsky *Marche des soldats de bois*

When considering this seemingly simple piano piece, it is worth remembering that Tchaikovsky was a master of the theatre who understood the magical world of childhood. Your pupil may well know the story and some of the music of *Nutcracker*. Perhaps the most remarkable thing about this soldiers' march is the subdued level of its dynamics. This tends to give distance to the music and conveys a mood of nostalgia, as though recalling happy memories from a bygone age. It is like gazing through a gauze curtain at a scene on stage.

However, rhythm and finger articulation will need nothing less than military precision. The hands need to drop lightly into the keys and then float off easily from chord to chord. The player is to shape the slurs carefully, keeping the dotted-note figures really crisp. Accents should be incisive but always contained within the prevailing quiet levels of tone. The slurred 3rds (bar 7 and similar) will need attention so that the notes are cleanly synchronized – the suggested fingering works well. If the staccato drum figure (see bars 8, 16 and 40) causes any difficulty, try tapping it on a rigid surface, watching how the finger and thumb have to spring up between each stroke. The alternating fingers, 1 and 2 (or 1 and 3 if preferred), help the hand to remain relaxed, and a useful exercise could be invented by repeating the pattern stepwise up and down a scale.

The metronome speed of crotchet = *c*.108 (some editions give a quicker tempo) is realistic for a march that requires character and clarity. These may be only toy soldiers, but we do not want them falling over each other.

B:3 Tarp *Sunshine*

The sunshine here is not the fierce heat of the Tropics or of recent European summers but rather the gentle warmth of a more temperate climate. Imagine sunlight dappling through leaves and the contentment of a lazy afternoon.

The phrasing and melodic shapes in this piece are reminiscent of Grieg's folksong style, and each bar has a natural rise and fall. The climax is marked by the highest notes of the right hand, in bar 5, and only here does the music flow on to make a two-bar phrase. The gentle mood requires delicate dynamics, with the loudest point being not much higher than *mezzo-piano*. Listen especially to the tenderness of the melody as it retreats into a shady *pianissimo* in bars 3 and 4 – the *una corda* pedal could be used here.

The left hand should be as legato as possible, and care will be needed to hold the long C♯ 'pedal' notes. If your pupil finds the stretches posed by the chords in the first two bars awkward, let the right hand help out. By moving the right hand's thumb back and forth between the top note of the first- and third-beat chords (G♯ dotted crotchet) and the melody A of the second and fourth beats, a very smooth effect can be achieved. This leaves the left hand with only 5ths and 3rds to manage.

At the end, the same rather awkward chord appears on the fourth beat (final cadence) and, as before, the G♯ can be taken by the right hand. In doing this a tiny break will occur in the melody line, which, if handled sensitively and incorporated into the *poco rit.*, can actually make an interesting musical point. Whatever means are chosen, the ending should just drift away as though dozing.

B:4 Hiller *Polish Song*

An expressive piece with some surprising moments of drama, this *Polish Song* requires independence of hands and a competence with different types of touch. The marked dynamics and articulation are very precise, and a reliable left hand is going to be essential. While the melody is found mainly in the right hand, it is the left that frequently drives the music forward, almost to the point of being argumentative during the middle section. In view of the nature of the music, the staccato should not be too short, the *forte* tone warm and unforced. Accents are used merely to emphasize special notes – they should not be overdone.

The phrasing for this piece is clearly marked. The repetition of melodic fragments and rhythmic patterns is typical of folksong style, but where a curved line is carried through several bars, a shapely, unbroken legato is desirable. The counter-melodies will need careful practice, especially those of the left hand in bars 12–24 and the plaintive comments of the right hand that follow. Persuading the independent voices to flow easily together will take time and patience. The final phrase then builds towards two bars of strong chords, defiant in character, only to subside into a mood of quiet resignation. The suggested metronome mark of quaver = 116 works well, but the player should feel an unhurried one beat in a bar rather than three.

For such a short piece, there is a wide range of emotions and ideas that will surely appeal to the pupil with imagination.

B:5 Niemann *Morgen im Walde (Morning in the Woods)*

The horn-like intervals, melodic shapes and cadences suggest a hunting scene and the title tells us of the wood where it is set. The mood is happy and the distant echoes add an air of expectancy and excitement. The pacing of the piece is going to be important, holding back just enough on the cadences marked *rit.* for them to make their point without bringing the music to a halt, and being able to resume the original speed at every *a tempo.*

It would be worthwhile taking the first three notes of the rising arpeggio theme with the left hand each time. This should reduce the risk of splitting notes, but it will also allow the player an enjoyable sense of freedom and encourage a shapely flourish as one hand passes to the other. Be bold, too, with the attack on the octave leaps in both hands at bars 9 and 11. Although an interrupted cadence is looming in bar 12, the left hand's awkward group of chords should keep in tempo; to slow down would pre-empt the approaching *poco rall.* For these same chords, the fingering 1/2, 1/3, 2/5 and 1/4 may create a smoother flow. Keep the left hand light and let both wrists rise a little as the group ends. The touches of pedal suggested in the score could easily cause blurring and add little to the overall effect. When in doubt, therefore, consider leaving them out.

Although this music presents a technical challenge, it paints such a vivid and exuberant picture that the practice needed to achieve success will be amply rewarded.

B:6 Stravinsky *Lento*

Stravinsky seems an unlikely composer of music for young pianists; much of his piano music is difficult, especially for small hands. However, his set of eight pieces entitled *Les cinq doigts* was specially written for children, presenting an opportunity to play something that is unmistakably Stravinsky and yet very approachable – technically and musically.

Lento is a sad, dance-like piece with a distinctly Russian flavour, its insistent rhythms perhaps suggesting the movements of puppets or marionettes. Each hand has its individual role to play. The right, restricted to the five-finger position of the title, is in D major while the left, seemingly unaware of its partner, plays a more solemn part in the minor mode. Both have irregular phrase lengths, an important feature of the music, so allowing a tiny 'breath' at the end of each group of notes will mark the phrasing.

If the left-hand slurs in bars 5–7 are too wide a stretch, consider applying a touch of pedal – to be released immediately on the staccato quavers. The accompaniment from bar 9 lies neatly under the hand if the fourth finger is placed on the D. The piece does not require a lot of dynamic contrasts, but the right hand needs a fuller singing tone than the left, and it sounds effective to start a crescendo on the repeated quavers in bar 9, towards the middle of the phrase. A rallentando is unnecessary at the end – indeed, it is more theatrical to give the impression of leaving the characters in 'mid-sentence'. A slight fade-out would do the trick.

In 1962 Stravinsky made an instrumental arrangement of these pieces (*Eight Instrumental Miniatures*). Here, *Lento* is given a metronome mark of crotchet = 63, but this may feel a shade slow for the piano version.

C:1 Bartók *Dance*

Bartók is often a favourite with teachers and pupils because of his rhythmic freshness and exciting harmonic language. This dance will be popular, but it is not without a few technical perils for the less confident pianist.

I would begin by practising the hands separately, starting with the left-hand chords. Pupils with a small hand and light arm will find it hard to play with the incisiveness, dynamic and energy required; this is particularly true of bars 18–20. The sound is best achieved from the wrist – with a firm bounce, the hand well supported and strong, active fingers. Crispness and rhythmic authority is essential, and the accent can be just a small 'kick' (nothing that will give the chord too much muddy length).

The folksong in the right hand also needs a decisive wrist staccato, with firmly rounded fingers. But the couplet phrasing may require some technical work (a down–up movement of the wrist here), and the accented crotchets will be achieved by dropping the wrist as the key descends – holding for the full length.

Note that while marks of articulation abound, the general dynamic level is limited in range. As the piece may need more than this, encourage a musical, dynamic shape to the phrases within the *mezzo-piano*. The final hurdle will undoubtedly be putting the hands together: an exercise in independence, it should be taken bar by bar and then phrase by phrase, just getting used to the movements and relationship between the hands.

There is much musical satisfaction to be had from a well-controlled performance. If topped with flair and character, this piece can really come to life.

C:2 Siegfried Merath *Cha-Cha*

A cheeky, slightly wicked cha-cha, this piece will not benefit from delving beneath the surface; instead, it will work well if imbued with a certain naivety – just playing exactly what is written. A quick demonstration of the dance would be good preparation, and plenty of films offer examples. Some mental image of the moves would greatly help in securing an idiomatic performance.

The piece should be learnt hands-separately at first – if only to build up the stamina needed to play the right hand staccato throughout. This staccato is best achieved with a light wrist action, using the weight of the hand, and at the key surface so that the movement is small and the tone light but precise. As so much is required of the fingers, good, consistent fingering is a must. Just a few small details of phrasing in the right hand add to the character, and I would shape the tune with a significant 'rise and fall' dynamically across the phrases. As an example, start *mezzo-forte*, crescendo towards the beginning of bar 2 and then diminuendo through the repeated Gs. The end of bar 8 and onwards could be a little more forte, dying away again in the laughing left-hand quavers in bar 16, for the return of the first theme.

The left hand needs good rhythmic security and should therefore be known as independently as the right hand, with all rests observed and the syncopation felt and internalized.

Separate work complete, the interplay between the hands will still need attention before it is comfortable; but if done slowly and intelligently, all will be well.

Pupils should enjoy the middle section, using a bolder tone; there should be strength enough in the sound to effect a dying away in the laughing quavers in bar 11 and similar. The final bar should be confident and fluent. Any fingering for the left-hand 5ths will do; you might prefer to use 1-4, 1-5, 1-4, 1-5. But however you arrive there, the final two notes should draw a smile from the audience.

C:3 Raymond Weber *Equivoque No. 8*

There are some pieces that are immediately evocative in their harmonies and sound-world. The wonderful C♮/C♯ contrast in the opening and mournful sigh of the right-hand phrase make this just such a piece. It should be played through several times to pupils, with perhaps a short description or some 'scene-setting' to draw them into the musical language and encourage them to play it.

The rewards for teacher and pupils alike are huge. From the teacher's perspective, the piece to be taught is technically relatively straightforward; there are no real demands except sensitive control of the musical shape. For the pupil, there is the joy of getting inside a piece that will live with them longer than might something more immediately appealing.

The piece is perhaps a soulful lullaby – a song with an accompaniment. The left-hand chords should be shaped in couplets, the first chord using a bit of weight, the second, very light. A gentle drop then lift of the wrist helps the sound.

The melody begins with two short phrases which also die away from the first beat, but this is followed by a longer two-bar phrase which could grow towards the top notes. Each subsequent two-bar phrase might then build towards the climax of bar 8. The tone should be well supported until the end of bar 12, after which it can die away.

Throughout the piece the left hand should be gentle and unobtrusive, with a little space allowed between each bar, except in bars 11–12 when the legato lines contrast with the gradually sleeping melody. The final chord is gentle, slower and peaceful.

C:4 Mike Cornick *Sue's Blues*

This is a wonderfully adolescent piece, and I suspect those with teenage children will relate immediately to the belligerent and grumpy, repetitive figures in the right hand.

As with many of the jazzy pieces in the early grades, this performance will rely heavily on a feel for the swing groove, a firm sense of pulse and a well-chosen tempo. Experience suggests that many accomplished performances will be played so fast that the piece will last less time than it takes to lift the pen. But, however admirable technically, these performances won't at all convey the appropriate mood, so pupils should be introduced to plenty of examples of the blues.

Crotchet = 108 is ideal – no faster – and from the outset, particularly in the second bar, the quavers should be swung (as if triplets), with the all-important 'push' or slight emphasis on the shorter note. It is difficult to describe how significant this can be, but listening to some Bill Evans will soon make the point. The E and F♯ at the beginning of bar 2 would have a slight accent, for instance; without this, the triplets at the bar's end would seem more like Mozart than Evans.

The left-hand chords should beat time like a gently tapping foot (in itself permissible in this piece, if quietly done). With so many repeated and rather 'moaning' phrases, variety in the dynamics will be all the more important in providing interest and character; crescendos should be graded carefully so that the tone never gets too robust or heavy.

The final, cheeky couplet should be played with a grin, the grace note light and 'tucked in', as if a final attempt to cheer things up. This is to no avail, though, as after a long pause the piece finishes with an understated, slightly mopey, bluesy chord.

C:5 Michael Finnissy *Tango*

Even with the most enthusiastic of introductions, scene-setting and imaginative performance, I suspect that most teachers will fail to attract all but the most adventurous and broad-minded of young pupils to this piece – but it is worth persevering.

It is an enormous shame that as young players progress through the early grades anything that strays from a strong sense of tonality is often condemned to the musical dustbin. This is all the more extraordinary considering that these very same pupils may have improvised atonal pieces representing elephants, thunderstorms and so on with great enthusiasm in their first lessons, their pieces providing complete musical satisfaction and enjoyment.

This piece cannot be played, however, without a strong sense of the character of a tango and a feel for the phrasing. Simply following the markings is a good start, but the articulation will need some repetition for hands to 'memorize' the gestures, particularly where there is a staccato/legato contrast (bars 1–2 and so on). Consistent and organized fingering with the minimum number of hand positions will help the memory and control. The 'relentless' applies to the rhythm (not to the sound world, which should be light), and the performance should follow the dynamics carefully.

A secure and definitive sense of pulse is an essential part of the character, as is a light and crisp, bright staccato in the right-hand chords and in the couplet phrasing.

The *forte* G in bar 22 should be counted carefully (long notes are notorious for being cheated of their full value in exams). Make the most of the quiet and cheeky ending to this slightly bizarre trip to the ballroom.

C:6 William Gillock *Flamenco*

Castanets at the ready, a quick strum of the guitar and stamp of the feet, and we are transported off to Andalucia, home of this dance. There is a humour and warmth to this sunny piece with an improvised 'song' in the middle and a hint of wild abandon at the end.

The opening will rely upon a firm, authoritative staccato in the left-hand chords – short but not too loud – and a lighter but clearly-phrased right hand. The tempo should be absolutely constant here, and the dynamics led by the left hand, reaching a vibrant 'strumming' *forte* in bar 17 (take note of the pedal marking) before calming to the *piano* and a very important bar's rest.

The most difficult section to bring off will be the middle 'song'. A bit more time and some rubato will be needed, as well as a brave holding-back of the marked pauses before the very Carmenesque triplet. Her famous aria comes to mind here, and I would strongly advocate listening to this or something similar to help capture the idiom.

The final section storms away and should arrive at the *fortissimo* in a frenzy. A very marked decrescendo over the next few bars will give the final chord and bass note their dramatic and humorous effect, with the dancers falling exhausted to the floor. Note the bar's rest at the end; this is a significant part of the piece, and the hands should be held over the keys before allowing the audience to clap.

A terrific piece for exams and concerts from the man who wrote the memorable *Swinging Sioux*!

GRADE 4

Many of the List B pieces will benefit from some pedal, but if legs are too short there is always an alternative piece from the extensive lists. The musical character of candidates often becomes more firmly established at this stage and they can play to their strengths, making sure the pieces are contrasted in tempo and mood.

A:1 J. C. F. Bach *Polonaise*

Picture the glittering scene of an eighteenth-century ballroom thronged with people. Imagine the beautiful gowns and dashing uniforms of the dancers, a blaze of colour as they glide and dip to the stirring strains of the opening processional – the splendidly flamboyant Polonaise.

The typical rhythmic patterns of bars 4 and 8, the repetition of figures and a firm emphasis on the second beat in the closing bars of each section (bars 8 and 18) are all characteristics of this dance. Your pupil must be positive with the dynamic contrasts. A bright, buoyant attack in *forte* should be employed and a light, but clearly projected, tone in *piano*, with every semiquaver crisply articulated.

Much of the supporting left hand can be lightly detached, but it creates interest to introduce some legato groups, especially when there is stepwise movement in the crotchets. For instance, in the first two bars it will sound effective to slur the second and third beats, even carrying the slur through to the first beat of the next bar. A natural break occurs when a note is repeated or where there is a leap.

Difficulty may be experienced with the unexpected intervals in the right hand of bar 7, and some beat-to-beat practice may prove helpful. It would be advisable to prepare the last two bars carefully too, as the mix of chromatic and diatonic notes in the final flourish needs to lie comfortably under the fingers. It is amazing how often a confident performance can falter a few beats before the end when that premature thought 'I've made it!' pops uninvited into the head. One of the most important lessons a player has to learn is how to concentrate up to and beyond the end of a piece.

A:2 Mysliveček *Divertimento in F*

The mood of this piece is appropriately amiable (*divertimento* means 'amusement') and rather cheeky at times, with its varied repetitions. Its relaxed tempo provides an admirable opportunity to cultivate an easy-flowing Alberti technique for the left hand. The player must listen carefully to the moving (melodic) bass notes and keep the repeated thumb notes murmuring gently in the background.

Given the piece's rondo form, the principal melody recurs several times, and only in the second episode (bars 29–44) is there a significant change of mood. In this passage the left-hand quaver upbeats are best detached, but the crotchets should be given full value. Throughout the piece, attention must be given to rhythmic detail; the dotted rhythms need always to be precise and crisp, and the semiquavers, triplet semiquavers and demisemiquavers all in ratio and underpinned by a steady pulse. Slowing down for difficult bars and speeding up over the 'easy bits' is a commonly heard mistake in the exam room, so it would be a good idea to practise sections of this with a metronome.

Teachers often believe that the hand must be lifted at the end of every slurred pair or group, and in many cases (bars 4, 9, 37 and similar) this is the musical thing to do; but in other places (such as bars 11, 29, 52) you might decide to let them flow without a break into the following note. Remember that the articulation and dynamics seen in Baroque and early Classical keyboard music are often added by the editor, so allow your ear to guide you and encourage your pupils to make their own decisions, too. They are more likely to remember the details if they do.

A:3 D. Scarlatti *Minuetto*

With its lively character and infectious good humour, this is sure to be a popular choice, and its brevity – without repeats it barely lasts more than half a minute – will only add to its appeal! The structure, texture and technical demands are all uncomplicated, and success is assured if your pupil has agile fingers and an understanding of Baroque keyboard style.

The articulation should be crisp, the best effect achieved by detached quavers and really sparkling semiquavers. If the suggested slurs are employed, they must be allowed to give impetus to the music without unduly accenting the first note of each pair; too many first-beat accents will only impede the flow and shape of the phrasing. The shift of the slurs to the second and third beats in bars 12–15 adds zest to the rhythm and will highlight the moving melodic notes. This passage hints at the minor mode for a few bars, so there is a danger of overlooking the G♯ in bars 16 and 17 when the major key is restored for the section's closing cadence. Care should be taken not to overlook the rests in the bass line in bars 12–15 and again in the second half.

As with the articulation, dynamic marks are editorial but work well, creating echo effects, and adding vitality and colour. The recommended metronome mark of dotted crotchet = 60 will ensure that this minuet dances along with a spirited one-in-a-bar lilt. At the end, a ritenuto is unnecessary – encourage just a tiny gap or 'breath' before the final note.

A:4 Beethoven *Rondo (Allegro)*

This light-hearted, jaunty rondo is a joy to play. Its key system – F major and closely related keys – means that the notes lie easily under the fingers. The beautiful minor section, meanwhile, affords an opportunity for contrast and expression.

Ultimately you will need a tempo that accommodates the rapid notes of the turn in bar 4 and gives the semiquavers of the second theme some agility, while allowing the lyricism of the minor episode to unfold expressively. A metronome speed of about crotchet = 108 would be suitable.

However, much more important than speed is the musical detail. The player must etch out the rondo theme with crisp staccato and lightly sparkling semiquavers against the quieter left-hand accompaniment. The dynamic markings, which are liberally dotted about, help to provide character and liveliness. The arpeggiated chord (bar 8) should not delay the flow of the melody; if it proves troublesome, encourage practice without spreading the chord until the phrase moves rhythmically. The tender theme of the minor section needs to be lovingly shaped, and in bar 58 a *poco rit.* would help to ease it back in again after a second (but related) theme has had its say.

The *ad lib.* allows for just that…to be free in time for a few moments. It would be a good idea mentally to remove the bar lines and let the shape of the phrase dictate how it is played. After lingering over the quavers, the player might regain speed gradually through the semiquavers so that he or she 'hits the ground running'. Whatever is decided, it is essential to find the original speed as the rondo theme returns for the last time.

A:5 Haydn *Finale*

A joyful, spirited piece that is sure to appeal to the confident pupil who likes to play fast. Musically uncomplicated, the piece nevertheless demands nimble fingers and the ability to control a light, clearly articulated Alberti bass. In these figures it helps to keep the thumb close to the key in order to restrict the volume of the offbeat repeated notes.

The mordents (the word means 'biting') must be crisp and on the beat, getting the melody off to an exuberant start, and the written-out ornaments in bar 42 are best thought of as acciaccaturas to avoid playing out of time. Elsewhere the trills should be measured, and in the recommended edition the (editor's) realizations for bars 6 and 25 are sensible given the *allegro molto* tempo. However, many may find that the suggested metronome mark of dotted crotchet = 72 is rather fast. A speed closer to dotted crotchet = 66 will still portray the exuberance of the movement while allowing musical detail and phrasing to be heard.

As an early example of Haydn's keyboard music, the piece should display uncomplicated but clearly contrasted dynamics – there is much scope for echo effects here. However, the eight-bar passage from bar 48, with its descending scales, could have a more expressive treatment, the tone falling away from the top notes each time.

In keeping with the style, too, many of the left-hand quavers should be lightly detached, but notice that several of the phrases end with crotchets (such as in bar 7 and at section endings); these will sound better given full value.

This is music to chase away the blues, and to escape from homework!

A:6 J. G. Krebs *Allegro in E flat*

Johann Gottfried Krebs was born into one of those musical families of which the most famous must be the great Bach dynasty. Today the Krebs are little known, but this sparkling miniature is an attractive addition to the repertoire.

Typical of early Classical keyboard style (the composer was some nine years younger than Haydn), this Allegro requires a bright attack and neat finger articulation. No dynamic marks are given, though it was customary to begin a lively piece *forte*. However, as the answering phrase (at bar 4) shifts the bass line an octave lower it will sound fuller; beginning *meno forte*, therefore, will give more impact to this feature. Encourage your pupil to decide which passages might be quieter and how the phrasing could be shaped by nuances. By its very nature, this cheerful piece requires a bold ending, but beware of too many changes in dynamics as the overall shape of the piece may be lost.

Some of the semiquaver patterns have inner melody notes (e.g. the F, G, Ab, G, F in the opening bars), shadowed by the left hand. Keep the repeated offbeat notes quieter here so that the texture remains transparent. Notice how the first and fourth semiquavers in bars 25 and 26 also form a melodic shape –from the Bb onwards these could all be played with the thumb, giving weight without effort. The wedge-like signs over notes are merely staccato marks, but some will need slightly more pointing (top notes, bars 13 and 14).

Quavers should be lightly detached throughout except for the right-hand one in bar 3 and the pairs at the end of each section; these need to be gracefully slurred.

Altogether, this is an attractive choice with few technical problems.

B:1 S. Heller *Prelude No. 28*

Warm and reflective, this Prelude tells a gentle yet colourful story and perhaps needs this as the basis for a successful interpretation. It is music for the more mature or exploratory pianist, one who can forge a connection between the notes and feeling. It requires a delicacy with tonal colour, an innate sense of rubato, but most significantly subtle balance between the hands.

Technically, it is balance that is the hardest aspect of the piece. The left-hand chords need to be gentle yet full and never intrusive, just a tender backdrop to the melody. In the opening this may not prove troublesome, but from bar 17 one note of these accompanying chords is taken by the right hand and specific work may be required to allow the melody to sing through. Some time spent playing the top fifth finger in bar 17 with a bright, firm tone while only half-depressing the lower F (with the thumb) will help finger independence. I would start with the thumb 'resting' on the key surface, then allow it to move a little, and so on. Once the physical sensation of the difference in touch is there, it should soon become second nature.

The middle section (bars 17–38) reveals a gradual change of character, a contrasting event. While pedal was needed for the opening section (changed on each left-hand chord), bars 27–32 require hardly any use of pedal, except perhaps a dab at the beginning of bars 29 and 30.

The melody itself should have lots of dynamic shading and a rhythmic pliancy to enable it to speak to the listener; this is best achieved if considered independently of the accompaniment, with the aim of maintaining the same effect once the chords are added.

B:2 Rebikov *Danse orientale*

This unusual and haunting piece presents few technical challenges for the grade, but it provides musical and rhythmic demands in abundance.

The first step is to get inside the music. The slinky motif that begins the piece, coupled with the more decisive steps of the minims, conjures up a colourful, jewel-bedecked dance with a hint of mystery. As such, the performance needs the right tempo – not too fast, to capture the sights, scents and sounds, yet not so slow that it loses its sense of dance. Too rhythmically exact and the performance will be deprived of character.

The opening quavers move away from the first note (not to be emphasized) with perhaps a slight accelerando into the quaver E of bar 2, before a fractionally delayed minim. Nothing too forceful is needed here as the minim's 'placing' will convey the tenuto and *mezzo-forte* by itself. The left-hand chords are soft, merely a backdrop to the melody, though note the rhythm in bars 4, 8 and so on, where the left hand could easily be placed a beat early.

The *più animato* should convey the more fluid movements of the dance. The music weaves around with plenty of dynamic shape to the line, the left-hand chords gently defined. Bar 35 onwards needs careful counting to indicate the rallentando while sounding 'in time'.

The dynamic range at the end needs planning as there is still a long stretch after bar 52. Ideally, there should be a gradual decrescendo throughout the last line, the final crotchet E being the softest note. For a good control of the sound as the scene fades into the background, decide jointly how softly the E can be played, and from that determine how firm the tone should be in bar 53.

B:3 Karganov *Arabesque*

Karganov's soulful yet beautiful music has a strong sense of 'smiling through your tears'. There is elegance yet melancholy to this Arabesque and two secrets to capturing both; one is balance, the other an instinctive and heartfelt use of rubato.

The potential problems are self-evident from the first two bars. The right hand's offbeat chords could easily make the music cumbersome and frantic, yet if played with the subtlest control they will simply add a gentle heartbeat and flow to the left-hand melody.

There is a distinct feel in the fingertips when producing the right sound here; fingers should be aware of, and use, the surface of the key with some arm weight to help the control. Any movement too precise or fast into the key will articulate the sound too boisterously, but flatter fingers 'drawn' along the surface with weight and a pliant wrist will work well.

In bars 3 and 4 roles are reversed, and it is here that some rhythmic freedom is essential. The left-hand jumps demand an easing of the pulse into the first beat of bar 4 – both to make the D expressive and to help the tonal control on the chords, which must be gentle, their bass notes carrying a touch more weight.

In bar 16 the *poco rit.* and crescendo must involve sensitive control of the final quaver-chord, which should be quieter than the F#, not intruding on the melody. There are greater musical and technical challenges in bars 11 and 15, where the accompaniment and melody have to be controlled within the same hand.

Pedalling must be judiciously considered. Bars 3–4 (and similar) will not work successfully without it, as the pedal holds the bass notes to give the harmonic richness. Elsewhere you can manage with very little pedalling, though more will make passages easier to play and will enhance the sound.

B:4 Grieg *Waltz*

Teachers often spend time helping pupils to differentiate between major and minor. This piece is a gift for them, the A major and A minor contrast being a feature throughout this attractive yet slightly reluctant waltz. This, together with the almost mazurka-like emphasis on the second beat and the mischievous ends to each section, gives this piece an unusual appeal.

The secret of an effective performance lies in light left-hand chords, careful pedalling and meticulous, well-defined articulation in the right hand. Small character details such as the switch of emphasis in bar 5 should be playful, 'placing' the tenuto E (just delaying it slightly), in this instance, with conviction. Bars 11–12 and similar need a quiet start and a crescendo to the middle of the phrase, with a bright staccato. The top notes of the chords should be clearly to the fore, with no stodginess in the lower parts; otherwise the piece loses all sense of the dance. Technically, the thumb of the right hand needs plenty of control and subtlety, while the fingers should be rounded, with active fingertips. It works to play notes with a quick, positive 'flick' along the key surface. The *subito piano* adds to the wry smile here and should be closely observed.

The middle section (imagine a violin solo with woodwind accompaniment) is to be equally well controlled and judged. Melodies should be worked out on their own musically, the dynamic shape and phrasing educated into the fingers until they are second nature. If such musical detail is included early on, the pupil will have memorized an aural 'pattern' with which to compare the tune when putting both hands together.

The coda should have space, warmth and poise, with a wonderfully teasing '?' at the end – the final major/minor contrast.

B:5 Gurlitt *Andantino con moto*

A somewhat elusive flower here; the petals seem reluctant to open in the morning sun yet finally blossom in the warmth, closing again for the evening.

The disjointed right-hand couplets will sound fragmented and lack direction if not treated carefully, both within the four-bar phrase and by themselves. Each couplet should be slightly louder than the preceding one until the top of the phrase is reached; within each couplet there is a slight lean into the first note, leaving the second one light and gentle.

The secret of this piece is in the wrist: the more pliant and 'giving' it is, particularly in the couplet 'appoggiaturas', the better the tone and the more likely the pupil will be to give that little expressive nuance. The wrist should fall with the first note, providing weight behind the finger, and then relax/rise in a circular motion for the second note, with a gentle lift – no harsh staccato here. Some rubato across the phrase is also needed. The grace notes, which come later, should be delicate and not intrude.

The sunny left hand really does need to be as legato and warm as the fingering will allow. An overlapping of the sound with the fingers (a physical legato) is needed, and, if comfortable, gaining a little help from judicious pedalling.

A good balance between the hands is important. The right hand is to the fore initially but the left-hand tune should come through from bar 9, confidently shaped, and with the right hand just attracting the ear briefly in bar 10.

If all the phrases begin quietly, there will be plenty of scope to colour and shape the line; any accents at the beginning of the phrase, or a too deliberate two in the bar, will spoil the overall sense of forward movement. Taking a little time across the final bar will help the control, and charm the listener.

B:6 Maikapar *Pastorale*

The challenge of this atmospheric piece is not so much the pronunciation of the composer's name as the rhythm of the opening and similar sections. The changes in time signature are not difficult, but it would be easy to mistake demisemiquavers for semiquavers in this piece, especially with the focus on note-learning.

The shepherd's-pipe opening should be learnt rhythmically at first, perhaps clapping through before adding the notes. This is only half the battle, however, as an improvisatory sense of the rubato within the pulse is needed, as well as confident and musical shading with dynamics. The faster notes at the end of the first and third phrases (bars 1 and 3) should be very delicate, and the echoing second and fourth phrases light throughout.

The two *più mosso* sections (Poco più mosso and Tempo II) are a little trickier than they first appear. A bold *mezzo-forte/forte* will promote the musical character as well as decisiveness in the articulation; the staccato is achieved with a small bounce at the wrist and on the ends of the fingers. Do not be put off by the slur-plus-staccato marks (*portato*) in the right hand of bars 21 and 22; the melody here is more legato than staccato.

The suggested dabs of pedal are not absolutely necessary. Indeed, they are perhaps rather fussy, and will not work on every piano or in every situation. Most of them, in addition, should be left out if the performer does not have an instinctive ear – otherwise conflicting harmonies may emerge.

The pressure of an exam performance may encourage pupils to hurry with the final bars. Full note-values in the penultimate bar and more than this in the final bar will provide the restful and reflective atmosphere needed. Consider 'placing' the final melancholy D minor chord.

C:1 Bartók *Melody in the Mist*

This piece is an excellent example of the use of opposing musical ideas. Based on tone-clusters, it depicts a misty atmosphere, indistinct and hazy, out of which emerge clear bold melodic lines like bright shafts of light.

Each chord consists of a perfect 5th encasing a minor 3rd, the left hand using all white notes and the right hand playing black notes (with the exception of B♮ in bars 26 and 36). Smooth lines, possibly with some overlap of sounds, will create the necessary 'creepiness' for the chords as they swirl around in semitones. Awareness of each note in the chord, always playing to the base of the key, will ensure that everything sounds. The contrast with the *forte* melodic phrases, played as single notes or in octaves, is striking; the tone here should be firm and confident, with a distinction made when the notes have tenuto lines (e.g. in bars 28–31).

Bartók's detailed pedalling links the two musical elements, by overlapping them. The long-held pedal in bars 39–43 creates a wonderful effect, especially when released for the final bar to reveal a bare octave G. A large hand may be able to hold the right-hand G in bar 39, playing the chords with the remaining fingers, but the left hand must rely on the pedal to hold its tied note; this should be re-depressed silently before releasing the pedal.

A reliable sense of pulse is essential, and care needs to be taken not to shorten dotted minims, especially when negotiating pedalling and changes of register. The metronome mark of dotted minim = 46 allows the piece to unfold in an unhurried, tranquil way.

C:2 Alan Haughton *Freeway*

The opportunity to have real fun should not be missed when preparing for an exam, and this attractive piece provides just that chance. It will sharpen up your pupil's rhythmic sense and be enjoyable to practise at the same time.

The metronome mark is very brisk, so the ability to move quickly is vital. Left-hand shifts in position in bars 5–12 need careful practice, and the player should strive for seamless movement between the hands at bars 3 and 19. Confident right-hand 3rds in bars 6 and 10 will help to ensure that the hands play exactly together.

An assured rhythm which flows naturally is the ultimate aim in this jazzy style. To sort out the rhythmic detail, encourage slow practice at 'feeling' four beats in a bar. Make sure that the left-hand quavers in bars 13–15 are accurately placed, and that the chord in bars 20–21 is held for its correct length.

The decisive character of this piece will be established immediately by a firm tone and clear staccato attack in the opening bars, and placing emphasis on the third chord in bars 2 and 4 will highlight the jazz rhythm. Make the most of the contrasts in dynamics, encouraging sufficiently quiet *piano* bars and observance of the crescendo–diminuendos. Notice, also, the accents in bars 16, 17 and 20, which give impetus to the rhythm. Pedal is not necessary for this piece, although occasional touches (e.g. from bar 20 to the short, quiet final chord) will help to enhance the phrasing.

C:3 Lutosławski *An Apple Hangs on the Apple-Tree*

Twentieth-century east European composers have been particularly drawn to arranging folk melodies for piano. This dance-like example, with its three-bar phrases and unusual left-hand patterns, is particularly attractive.

The first four bars act as an introduction to the folk tune that enters at bar 5. Four three-bar phrases, with alternating dynamic levels, comprise the main body of the piece, while a coda (beginning bar 17), similar to the introduction but at different octaves, rounds things off.

Learning notes should not be a problem due to the considerable repetition of phrases, but confidence is required to secure the left-hand leaps, especially in bars 5–7 and 17–19. The use of different registers of the piano necessitates body movement from side to side (while still sitting on the stool!); this applies especially to bars 17–19, where three octaves are covered. The changing of fingers for the right hand's repeated semiquavers, while not obligatory, will help clarity, especially at *pianissimo* level.

The tempo should reflect the *moderato* marking, and thinking one-in-the-bar will give buoyancy to the dance rhythms. A firm *forte* establishes the mood at the start, but the diminuendo and ritardando in bars 3–4 (with silence at the pause) require careful pacing to prepare for the melody. Clear dynamic contrasts, using a very quiet *pianissimo* tone, will highlight the three-bar phrase structure of bars 5–16, and the folk character can receive emphasis by stressing the second beat of bar 7 and similar. The unexpected ending, which disappears to nothing, is highly effective in its inconclusiveness.

C:4 Philip Cashian *Slow Moon*

Most pupils enjoy depressing the pedal and exploring sonorities over the whole keyboard (often the more dissonant the better!), so this piece, an excellent introduction to contemporary piano writing, should appeal to the creative, enterprising player. The style is almost improvisatory. The music is timeless and mysterious, so imagining a calm scene, vast yet gentle, will help to create the right mood.

Good freedom of arm movement and keyboard geography are essential, but, although the notes may appear daunting, the 'lazy and unrushed' tempo gives time for moving around the piano. The composer uses repeated note-patterns, and it will be beneficial to 'spot' these during the early stages of learning, taking note of any changes of clef. Leger lines will need accurate reading, and care should be taken with the *8ve* signs in bars 5, 7 and 17 (applying only to the Eb). The chords at beat one in bars 13 and 15 will be easier if fingered 4/1 – 5/2 in both hands.

Although there is a spacious, unhurried atmosphere here, a clear sense of pulse is necessary for conveying the overall shape. The changes of time signature in bars 13–18 need care, so that semiquavers are played on, not before, the beat. The tricky rhythm at bars 20–22 will not cause problems provided the player has a clear understanding of where the main crotchet beats occur.

Dynamics are indicated sparingly, most of the piece being marked *piano* or *mezzo-piano*, but the short-lived climax at bars 15–17 should be relished. Holding the pedal as marked (but with clear changes) will help to create wonderfully clashing sounds, and using *una corda* will add further colour to the final bar, which may be held *a niente*.

C:5 Kabalevsky *March*

Kabalevsky wrote numerous attractive pieces for the aspiring pianist, most incorporating technical points within a musical setting. Many pupils have an aversion to practising 'studies'. This sprightly march, however, will prove a most effective and enjoyable vehicle for developing good staccato.

A successful performance will require facility across the keyboard and confident rhythm. But the lively character suggested by the *allegro* marking can be achieved also by well-contrasted dynamics, clear accentuation and crisp staccato – without attempting a dangerously fast tempo.

Quick thinking is the key to anticipating the frequently-shifting hand positions over the black keys. In addition, quaver practice in legato, once fingerings have been worked out, will help establish reliable patterns. Memorizing some 'corners' may be necessary so that the keyboard can be glanced at, for accuracy.

Either finger or hand (wrist) touch, keeping close to the keys, may be used for staccato; some initial staccato practice at different dynamic levels, perhaps on a scale or five-finger exercise, may prove beneficial.

The piece falls into three sections (the first and third being identical), preceded by a short fanfare-like introduction and ending with a coda. Clear dynamic levels with audible crescendos and accents will give interest to the main outer sections (bar 5 onwards). The contrasting middle section (bars 29–36), meanwhile, can be characterized by semi-staccato and short touches of pedal on the left-hand slurs.

In this music, rhythmic stability is of paramount importance; isolating awkward leaps and practising slowly (then gradually increasing the pace) will help to build the confidence necessary to perform this challenging but appealing piece.

C:6 Elizabeth Maconchy *The Fair*

A busy rural fair, perhaps as in a Brueghel painting, is conjured up in this piece. The outer sections of the ternary structure suggest a peasant dance with stamping feet and plenty of jollity, while the music of the central 3/8 section, which is generally quieter, seems to explore more personal thoughts.

The crotchet pulse must remain constant during the alternating time signatures, and care should be taken to maintain the quaver speed at the change to 3/8 in bar 7 (subdividing the previous 3/4 bar into quavers will help). Tempo I, after the *poco rall.*, should match the opening tempo.

In the outer sections, a loud incisive attack, with all semiquavers detached, will immediately characterize the dance. Firm second-beat accents can be enhanced further by the pedal, lifting on the first beat of the next bar. The leaps need careful practice – and attempted with eyes closed, to improve judging distances! Note that the right-hand F♯ carries through bar 4.

Careful fingering of the left-hand chords in the 3/8 section in order to create legato is important; this may need modifying for a small hand, but the chords should be linked in twos, joining at least the lowest note. Also in this section, right-hand staccato with phrase marks (*portamento*) will yield longer, more lyrical sounds than elsewhere in the piece. A clear idea of where the climax occurs will give direction to the section, and shaping of individual phrases will be enhanced by an appreciation of the colourful harmonies.

Leave deciding whether or not to make a ritardando in the final bars to the performer; either will work!

GRADE 5

School exams often become a serious threat to practice around Grade 5, so forward planning is helpful to ease the pressure. The preparation time for this grade will need to be longer than for the previous grades, but some light pieces that are quick to absorb will help to maintain enjoyment in playing while the exam work is being systematically covered.

A:1 Handel *Gigue*

It is difficult to imagine this buoyant and confident Gigue in any other key as it sits for the most part so well under the hand. Dancing away with bold arrogance, the piece has always a twinkle in the eye.

Performing the piece successfully requires the same confidence and absolute technical assurance. This begins with some fastidious attention to notes and, most importantly, fingering. Lots of separate practice of hands is needed in the early stages.

Knowing quite what fingering to use is hard before the phrasing is considered, so this may be the best place to start. You might consider, at least in the first few bars, the editorial suggestion of slurring the first two quavers of each 'triplet'. In bars 5 to 7, however, this could lead to too many strong beats, so keep the second- and fourth-beat triplets staccato to give a two-in-a-bar feel. In bar 19, having slurred the first two quavers I would keep all subsequent quavers short. With articulation decided, the fingering should become simpler. Encourage careful use of the fingers to ensure that the parts are clearly defined.

It is small musical considerations that will make the difference between a matter-of-fact, perhaps clumsy rendition and something with poise and character. Bright upbeats (whether on a single note or a bar's last two right-hand quavers) are essential, as are light upbeat quavers in the left hand. Think the dynamics in long phrases; make a gradual decrescendo through bars 2 and 3, for instance, getting softer in bar 5 before a crescendo in bar 6. Attention to details such as the held dotted crotchets in bar 9 and the left-hand rests in bar 17 will also contribute to a stylish performance.

Finally, spend some time deciding on an appropriate tempo. Much will depend on the pupil's technical ease, and the degree of subtlety employed to shade and articulate the piece; but the chief consideration will be the semiquavers in bar 2.

With the right preparation, a good ear and a keen sense of the music's character, this Gigue will come across as a wonderfully joyous piece.

A:2 Hook *Rondo*

This cheerful, happy-go-lucky Rondo provides many of the same musical challenges as the Handel Gigue, but within an easier technical framework. The opening bubbles away like a good champagne, buoyed up by a bassoon-like left hand. The 'Minore' moves around a little less in register, and speaks its mind in a rather sombre manner until a return to the major is heralded.

Technically, there is only one major hurdle – that of even semiquavers played with ease and musical shape. Lots of rhythmic practice, accents on offbeat notes and staccato work will all pay dividends, as will, at every stage, measured use of dynamics; these must be a part of the performance as much as notes and fingering. Phrases are virtually all four bars. In the opening, a bold start might be followed by a slight decrescendo in bar 2 then a rise and fall from bar 3 to bar 4. A dynamic 'arc' through bars 9–12 works well, and the block dynamic contrast towards the end of the first section (bars 17–20) is worth making.

At no point should the slightly subservient left hand be neglected. Intelligently considered and well-articulated shape and phrasing will greatly enhance the performance here. Notes are never just staccato, and each note can be more or less shorter than the previous one; this gives a chance to point and shape each phrase with great subtlety. Treat the left hand as its own melody and be happy only when it has a musical identity as strong as that of the right hand.

In the middle section the change of mood and dynamic should be clearly defined. There is a danger that the left-hand chords might be too forceful and robust, so they should be played with a pliant wrist and well-judged tone.

There is much to enjoy in this piece, and much to convey. The charm, humour and contrast will not come through in the notes alone, and it must really be 'sold' by the performer.

A:3 Kirnberger *Les Carillons*

This characterful piece is a lively Bourrée, but not just in its style and structure. The performer's fingers and hands will, in fact, take a lead role on the dance floor, judging from the acrobatics of bars 13 and 14. The piece therefore needs a confident and assured performance, by a well-prepared pianist who has some natural flair and a fluency around the keyboard.

Begin by learning both hands independently as if both were the melody, writing in all fingering and deciding upon the phrasing. In general, all crotchets will be detached, dotted crotchets and minims long, and quavers either legato or slightly articulated, depending upon personal preference.

To keep the performance on its toes, particularly in the opening section, encourage your pupil to think two-in-a-bar and of a light second (minim) beat. This will mean that every bar has one main emphasis. Bar 2 might, therefore, have a slightly longer first crotchet, with the remaining crotchets becoming lighter and shorter to help the phrase move forward.

In the acrobatic bars 13 and 14 the top As should be lighter than the bottom notes. The final three left-hand crotchets of each bar from bar 17 might be shaped towards the first beat, to avoid too disjointed a sound.

The 'Alternativement' works well at a slightly more relaxed tempo. There are expressive moments within the melody, such as the written-out appoggiatura (the E of bar 22, for instance), and the melodic lines from bar 33 are more legato and eloquent. To enhance the more lyrical nature of this trio and its melancholy mood, the left-hand crotchets should be lengthened and just slightly detached.

The suggested dynamic contrasts add an effective vividness to the performance, the *forte* from bar 29 communicating the major key and a brighter sound. Within these dynamics, however, a full and varied range of colour is needed, with balance playing a significant part; the left hand should never be too forceful.

After all this preparation it is important to let go and perform with panache, the hands leaving the keys with confidence and dancing their way throughout.

A:4 Clementi *Allegro*

This cheerful sonata movement will appeal to those pupils whose left hand does not yet match the control, dexterity or easy technique of their right. This is music that should be played with happiness in the melodic line; phrasing should be carefully shaded, the articulation clean and sprightly.

The left hand provides little more than a rhythmic harmonic accompaniment; if it is too robust, it may destroy any melodic personality or charm.

The chords should be light – fingers close to the keys with a supple wrist. In accompanying figures such as those from bar 16 the bass note should have some moral fibre, the subsequent chords lightening as the bar progresses (the articulation gentle, not too staccato).

With the right-hand melody, it is most important to identify the phrase length and shape, as this will dictate the dynamic level at any point. The repeated Gs in bar 4, for instance, cry out for a decrescendo through the bar; the semiquavers in bar 5, despite the *forte* marking, need initially a subtlety and lighter touch, so that the phrase can move through this bar and to the next with dynamic shape and direction. A *subito forte* or accent on the first note would stop any sense of flow.

Similar control is needed in all upbeat semiquaver groups, as in bar 8, and also at the ends of phrases where there needs to be a beautiful lightening of the final quavers (bars 20 and 28, for example) – something, alas, rarely heard.

Dynamics need the performer's full and undivided attention throughout. Could a listener guess the intended dynamics just from hearing the performance? If not, more contrast is needed.

The buoyant articulation should include short and light staccato upbeats. The hands' 'choreography' plays a crucial part in this, and the natural movement of the wrist and fingers will help the articulation and shape.

Finally, don't neglect the rests. These are an important part of the texture (or lack of it) and, right through to the 'semi-colon' three bars before the end, they can convey as much of the character of the piece as the notes do.

A:5 Kuhlau *Allegro con spirito*

This is a typically buoyant and lively sonatina movement from Kuhlau. This composer's obsession with turning scales into vibrant, exciting melodies raises a smile, but it also creates frustration as fingers get into a tangle. If your pupil has difficulty playing scales evenly, with consistent fingering, then this piece should be avoided for an exam; it can be learnt instead as repertoire. Conversely, for those prepared to spend time consolidating fingering, and who have both a good memory for fingering patterns and a natural control and articulation, this piece is a gift.

Central to a convincing performance is making musical magic out of melodies that could easily sound like exercises. The opening phrase, for instance, needs a light, bright touch, the top line to the fore, the thumb not intruding. There should also be a charming shape throughout, with the 6ths rising or falling in dynamic level. The tied notes are held for their full length, with a gentle left-hand pizzicato in the background.

Any excessive use of pedal will destroy the music's charm, so a good, fingered legato is crucial. The suggested fingering gives pupils plenty of choice in articulation. The 3rds in bars 5 and 6 should perhaps be legato, likewise those in bars 30, 31 and so on.

The left hand is at its most dangerous in places such as bars 13–16 where it might easily 'count time' in march fashion. Avoid excessive hand rotation here as this could result in a persistently intrusive thumb. Aim instead for a more legato and perhaps even sustained lower part, gently lifting the chords in time to play the next one.

Forte markings at the beginning of runs are not accents but could readily be interpreted as such by clumsy hands. A forgiving wrist and keeping the tone up for most of each phrase will help here.

With all the right ingredients – technical assurance, the well-articulated phrasing light and colourful – this sparkling and joyful sonatina will be fun to play and a pleasure to listen to.

A:6 Scarlatti *Sonata in A*

This is a coquettish and playful sonata full of charm and smiles. Essential to a convincing performance is a simplicity and poise which will entail some thorough technical grounding and control. It is often the case that passages requiring the most concentrated work should, in the end, sound the easiest to the listener; all that hard work and none of the recognition! If there is no comment on how tricky the piece is, the player has definitely succeeded.

The first step to learning this piece must be an in-depth exploration of tone quality, phrasing, articulation and tempo. Notes learnt with too heavy a touch or without the musical phrasing will have to be relearnt later, so it is far better, during slow practice, to adopt the correct articulation and shaping straightaway. Remember that all staccato hand movements must be just as short as they would be at tempo – slow practice to be done with a fast mechanism.

Only a very little arm-weight is required to help the tone and dynamic shape, and upbeats should be kept very light. For the right hand, it is important to understand the phrase lengths – this will help greatly in considering the dynamics. The first two phrases are two bars long (note the editorial commas, which are not pauses for breath but structural markings). The third phrase, however, stretches unusually and exquisitely over six full bars; this is a surprise and a delight, requiring some careful grading of the dynamics to lead the listener through to the final cadence. Echoes work well in bars 11–14, and a long crescendo can be made from bar 19.

There are some very expressive moments not to be missed, mostly centring on appoggiaturas. Lingering a little over these will highlight the wonderful dissonance they create. An instinctive understanding of these is difficult to cultivate, but if the right hand is put an octave lower in bar 7, for instance, the expressive poignancy becomes self-evident. The effect is heightened in bar 60 where the resolution is on to the unison – a magical moment. Throughout the piece, the left hand is generally to be played detached.

With subtlety, care and lightness of touch, this sonata makes for a particularly charming choice.

B:1 Bloch *Dream*

'A good dream and deep' are words of Hilaire Belloc which sum up this beautiful piece. The ambiguous and ever-shifting tonality finally settles in G major, as the dream comes to a peaceful close.

Clear balance of tone is a key element throughout the piece. Melodic interest shifts between the hands, so careful listening will be needed to project the appropriate line – passing, for instance, from the right hand to the left in bars 14–15. Firm yet flexible tone will give presence to the melodic phrases. The accompanying quavers, meanwhile, require careful control, keeping the fingers close to the keys and using the minimum of movement. The right hand in bars 12–14 contains both tune and accompaniment, and it is important to differentiate between the two roles.

Thinking three main beats in a bar will help the piece to flow, and the dream-like character suggests considerable rhythmic flexibility. Some unexpected harmonies occur between bars 19 and 30, so care should be taken to hold accidentals through the bar, especially the right-hand G♯ in bar 23. Left-hand ties in bars 15–21 should be accurately observed. The changes of harmony can be savoured; the transition to bar 22 and the shift to G major in bar 31, both enhanced by ritardandos, are particularly lovely.

A subtle range of quiet dynamic levels is explored, with the tone only ever reaching *mezzo-forte*. Tenuto lines indicate the most important notes within phrases, and a distinction should be made between *piano, più piano* and *pianissimo*.

The pedal helps to sustain the texture, and good synchronization – releasing the pedal fully and at the right time – is essential for clean harmonic changes. The choice of when to pedal is left to the individual, though the final G major section contains bass notes which can only be sustained by the pedal. Experimentation, changing on each new chord pattern, will provide the clue to good pedalling.

B:2 Lyadov *Bagatelle No. 1*

This short, Chopinesque piece, packed with musical interest and charm, will be best for a mature player with good tonal and rhythmic flexibility. It consists of two eight-bar phrases, the second a variant on the first, with each moving from G♯ minor to B major.

Although short, this piece is not a simple option, since considerable confidence, together with flexibility of the hand and wrist, is needed to negotiate the figuration which hovers over the black keys. The notes are mostly diatonic within B major, but the player should note the double sharps in bars 2, 4, 9 and 10. Practising the right hand alone without pedal will highlight the need for finger legato; small breaks may be necessary for a small hand (the leap of a 7th in bar 1, for example), but pupils should endeavour to play as smoothly as possible before adding pedal. The left hand provides stability over which the right hand weaves its magic; pedalling in whole bars, changing on each first beat, will preserve the whole harmony. The progressions can be further enhanced by slightly emphasizing the first beat, and projecting the thumb minims in bars 4, 6, 12 and 14 will create extra interest within the texture.

A convincing rubato (the life-blood of this style) will require gentle moving forward and pulling back of the quavers; at the same time, recognizing bars 5 and 13 with their second-inversion harmony as the focal point of each phrase will give impetus and direction. The quaver anacrusis at the start should not be lengthened to a crotchet, and the triplets, from bar 9, will need accurate spacing in relation to their neighbouring quavers.

The undulating melodic line offers plenty of scope for gradual dynamics, despite the piece not being very loud. *Dolce* implies a sweet, perhaps even dream-like quality in the right hand, especially for the triplets in bars 9–11. A meltingly subtle diminuendo in bars 14–15 will prepare for the final B major chord.

B:3 Burgmüller *La Tarentelle*

This piece conjures up a lively Mediterranean folk dance, all bustle and merriment. The villagers assemble during the eight-bar introduction, before the main dance begins at bar 9. At bar 33 the change to D major heralds a second dance, with contrasting steps, after which – with the repeat of the theme of bar 9 – the dancers return to the first dance. Perhaps the villagers run out of sight from bar 60, and the band announces the end of the merrymaking in the last three chords.

The tempo must capture the two-in-a-bar feel. At the same time, a wise candidate will choose a speed which allows clarity in the repeated notes and neat synchronization of the hands. A firm pulse should be maintained throughout, resisting the tendency to rush in the excitement of this music, especially at the rests in bars 5–8 and during crescendos. Although not obligatory, the printed fingering will aid rapid note-repetition (for instance, at bars 41–4), which is often difficult on an unfamiliar piano. The coda (bar 56 onwards) may require additional practice in the right-hand in order to move confidently up the keyboard. Good fingering for the left-hand chords will ensure correct notes at speed, and practising the quavers in bars 21–4 as three-note chords should help establish hand shapes.

Slurring from a weak to a strong part of the beat, in for example bars 17–22, requires a light arm and flexible wrist for the second note to be lifted while preserving the correct accentuation. Slow practice will help fit the right-hand slurs over the smooth left-hand quavers in bars 21–2.

The main melodic interest is in the right hand, so careful listening is needed to ensure a quieter left-hand tone that will support, not overpower, the tune. Well-shaped quavers in bars 1–4 and sudden drops to *piano* at bars 17 and 33 will create excitement, and the ending will be most effective if the tone disappears to almost nothing before the final chords, which are back in tempo after the *poco rit.*

B:4 Gade *Boys' Merry-go-round (Ringeltanz)*

This character piece should prove a real 'winner' with pupils who enjoy moving quickly around the keyboard. The music is attractive throughout and in addition contains many useful technical ingredients for pianistic development.

Neat crisp fingerwork and clear phrasing are needed to allow the energetic, boisterous character of the A minor sections to project. Clear accentuation in bars 1–2 (with the accents on the first, not third, note of each slur) will establish the two-in-a-bar pulse that is essential to this dance. Care must be taken not to cut short rests, for instance in bars 4 and 8. The speed of the right-hand scales in bars 3–4 and 7–8 may be faster than is usually expected for Grade 5, so encourage practising ascending scales at a rapid tempo and listening for neat, unobtrusive thumb notes. Use of the pedal as indicated adds warmth to the texture and underlines the phrasing, but careful synchronization is required to ensure clean changes of harmony in bars 9–11.

Perhaps the girls join in the boys' merriment for the middle section (bars 19–30), only to be cast aside at bar 31! Really quiet playing is seldom well done in an exam situation, but a clear drop in dynamic level at bar 19 (with even quieter left-hand chords) will immediately set the more tender mood, even though this is interrupted by *forte* four bars later. The chords in the left hand need careful fingering and practice – guard against muddling accidentals in bars 19, 26 and 27. Identifying common notes in successive chords (the thumb, for example, plays E throughout bars 25 and 26) will help pupils memorize finger patterns.

The final two-bar phrase, with its hemiola (an impressive word for any pupil to learn!), is most effective when played strictly in time, as the boys' game disappears into the distance.

B:5 Glière *Sketch (Esquisse) in D*

A piece without a title allows the imagination free rein in its creation of a picture or mood. A carefree ramble in gently undulating countryside on a perfect summer day is one idea which springs to mind; this may not appeal to all pupils, however, so they should be encouraged to explore their own thoughts and images in order to produce a really convincing account.

Gajamente means 'sprightly'. The two-plus-three crotchet pulse, with its irregular two main beats, gives a rhythmic lopsidedness which is both attractive and unusual. Counting in crotchets may be necessary at first to ensure that minims are not cut short, especially in bars 18–25. Eventually, however, we must think two-in-a-bar, to create the required momentum.

The written notes look relatively straightforward. But the brisk tempo, which should perhaps be gauged by the quavers in bars 41–3, may cause patterns to be learnt inaccurately, especially the changes of position in bars 35–41. Sorting out ties and slurs within a bar (as in bar 6) needs a keen eye and ear.

Sensitive shaping of the mellifluous tune will give added interest. Imagining different instruments playing various lines can prove stimulating, especially to a pupil who is learning an orchestral instrument also – you might imagine a French horn at the start, and violins and cello from bar 41 to the end. A challenge to all pianists is balance of tone – playing accompanying notes or chords quieter than the melodic line. Here, the tune is mainly in the right hand, shifting to the left in bars 19–22 and 41–3. Singing and playing the tune without the surrounding texture will establish what is melodically important. Other methods for practising this balance might include pupil and teacher playing tune and accompaniment, as a duet, or pupil playing the melodic line while 'ghosting' silently the accompanying notes, always with an emphasis on listening.

The suggested pedalling in bars 6–10 can be applied the whole way through; some bars, for instance 27–8 and 41, may be pedalled throughout, but most will require two changes to preserve harmonic clarity. A carefully graded diminuendo at the end, perhaps holding down the pedal through the final two bars, will bring the piece to a gentle close.

B:6 Heller *Study in A flat*

Many pupils associate studies with mechanical, repetitious practice, but here is an expressive piece worthy of the concert hall. The mellow key of A flat major combined with imaginative pianistic writing make this study a joy to work on and perform.

The piece provides a good opportunity to explore 'rubato', that nebulous concept that is difficult to define but satisfying to indulge in! A convincing style of rubato must come from within, prompted, perhaps, by discussion of where to move forward or pull back. To begin with, most players need to exaggerate the elasticity of the pulse before being able to temper their ideas within the overall rhythmic structure.

There are four main sections, each with subtle variations, and a coda. The crossing of hands requires freedom of arm movement and confidence over the keyboard, especially for the two-note slurs in bars 23–5 (it is possible to rearrange this pattern to avoid hand-crossing, but as printed is more fun!). The right-hand chords spanning the octave, in bars 35 and 36, can be played taking the lowest note with the left hand, and the sustained right-hand thumb notes, in much of the piece, may be held by the pedal. A two-in-a-bar flow should be maintained throughout, with no slackening of pulse at the triplets in bars 27–9 (take care to place the left-hand semiquaver accurately within the triplet).

Pedalling is necessary to enhance the harmonic texture and to join chords and wide leaps, listening carefully for clean changes. Savouring the colourful harmonies and expressive treble notes will make sense of the detailed dynamic markings, which often direct interest towards the second beat. The modulation to C minor at bar 21 heralds a short-lived climax that needs real energy and conviction.

C:1 Gillock *New Orleans Nightfall*

If there is one piece that will be a hit on the syllabus, then this is sure to be it! Quite rightly so, since young players and their relatives will enjoy this beautifully written blues that cries out to be rhythmically swung – in a 'song style; somewhat flexibly'. The dotted quaver and semiquaver rhythm can be interpreted as crotchet and quaver with a triplet sign underneath.

The outer sections are relaxed and easy-going, and the middle section is nearly three times as fast. In this contrasting section imagine the solo instruments of a big band playing the single-line melodies, while the whole band plays the brassy chords with their accents and *sforzandi*. On the return to the slower section the playing should have a more pronounced beat; the pulse itself should be strict, though of course the swung rhythm may continue.

All of the bass-clef chords indicate that the right hand is to play the top note or, sometimes, as in bar 9, the top two notes. Since jumping down to these notes and then back up to the melody involves wide leaps, the student needs a great deal of physical freedom, and the ability to pedal so that the sounds can be sustained. At the return of the opening tempo (bar 21) watch out for the melody lines in unison; hands here are *two* octaves apart and the octave sign above the right hand (top line) can readily be missed. Also, on the fourth beat of bar 31, note that the final C at the top of the bass chord is tied until the very end.

The dynamics, which are clearly marked, build towards the climax at bar 25, then draw us back down to the final *pianissimo* and ritardando at the end. Could the paddle-steamers be disappearing down the Mississippi during the last two bars, the blues melody echoing faintly into the distance?

C:2 Villa-Lobos *Adeus, bella morena!*

This sorrowful piece demands independence of the hands throughout, and would suit the player who enjoys the more melancholy side of music-making. In this piece of four sections (ABCA) there are many repeated phrases, so an imaginative approach to the dynamics is required. There are also many changes of tempo to be observed, and if the phrasing's natural ebb and flow is to be projected, it is essential that the moves to *a tempo* and *muito animado* after a slowing of the pace are handled with consummate ease.

Setting a relaxed but steady tempo at the start is important. From the outset the right-hand melody is played legato against a chordal left hand; in section C (bars 33 to 48) the roles are reversed. The left-hand quaver chords should be lightly detached and not heavy, and inevitably some pupils will find this touch difficult to execute. Encourage them to transfer the weight across the keys from one chord to the next with a floating arm, to avoid getting stuck in the keys. They may find this touch easier to apply to chords in the right hand, so section C could be practised first to acquire the movement, and then copied by the left hand for the other sections.

The *mezzo-forte* of the opening needs some rise and fall within the phrasing to avoid a rather bland sound. In bar 11 the repetition of bar 9 could be softer, before the intensity increases with the end of the first section. Section B begins *forte* in G major and is therefore a brighter sound. The left-hand chords, at a more animated tempo, are even shorter and suggest a folksong style – perhaps the music recalls happier times with the dark-haired beauty of the title.

Section C may present problems of co-ordination. The left hand's grace note needs to be lightly tucked into the melody line, and both hands must be carefully balanced. The repeat of the A section could begin *piano* and increase to *mezzo-forte* at the *a tempo* in bar 57, before descending to *piano* for the last statement of the doleful melody.

C:3 Richard Rodney Bennett *Diversion No. 5*

These days busy children are often in search of a quick fix as regards learning a piece, and the brevity of this piece – with six bars out of the total 25 repeated – will be very appealing. But beware! Within this pianistic little piece there is much detail of articulation and dynamic variety which needs to be incorporated with skill. It will suit those players in particular who have nimble fingers and a crisp touch.

The metronome mark (given by the composer) indicates a fast tempo, to be played with vigour and a non-legato touch. Dotted quavers and semi-quaver patterns, therefore, should not be slurred but separated by the slightest of gaps, a whisker of air. For the correct effect, imagine dabbing the keys. Staccatos, on the other hand, must be very short, and need to be played with the utmost precision.

To help maintain consistency in the touch, consider a different fingering from that marked for bar 5 (and 21): make the right hand's dotted quaver A a third finger, not a thumb. This will involve a series of quick thumb movements over bars 4–5, but it may prevent disturbance to the repeated dotted-note pattern.

The character of this miniature will be found when the dynamics are carefully judged and meticulously observed. There is a lot of detail packed into a small number of notes! Finally, the crescendo at the end brings the piece to its climax; the fingers must be strong, throwing off the last bar with aplomb.

C:4 Cuong Nguyen *Ostinato*

'Ostinato', meaning 'obstinate' or 'persistent', was usually teamed with the word 'basso' in the Baroque era (*basso ostinato*, literally 'ground bass') and used as a form of variation; in other words, a short bass phrase was repeated many times beneath varied upper parts. This contemporary composer has embraced that idea, and while the bass line is not repeated exactly, the repeated Eb/Db figure has been used to create a piece with a decidedly stubborn character.

The metronomic evenness of the quaver is essential. If this is achieved, then the 7/8s and 5/8s should take care of themselves. There is, however, potential for an accidental stretching to 6/8 from bars 18 to the end, if strict rhythm is not maintained. The last bar in particular needs to be exact; it kicks off in a cheeky jazzy style, with, as the composer says, no ritardando beforehand. Instructions for dynamic changes are clearly given (the climax comes in the middle of the piece), but remember to maintain the *forte* in bar 12 until the change into 5/8 at bar 18. Care should be taken never to allow a percussive sound, even on the accented octaves in bars 12 and 13. At this point a strong sound will be achieved by placing the hand on to the octaves, preparing with a lift from the upper arm and subsequently dropping the weight of the arm (at the same time supported by firm fingers). The concluding diminuendo, five bars from the end, should not be overlooked.

The piece lies well under the hand, but a helpful fingering for the beginning would be 3/1 then 2/1 in the right hand, to shape the hand ready for finger 3 in bar 2. This hand position can be returned to later in the piece.

This exciting punchy piece represents a great choice for the student who has a strong sense of rhythmic drive and energy.

C:5 Peter Sculthorpe *Song for a Penny*

This piece, according to the composer, recalls the 1930s machine that was the forerunner of the jukebox, and the kind of popular music that was played on it. The opening two-bar introduction sets the scene and transports us back into this era. This is a delightful singing piece that should appeal to most teenagers, and it is likely to be one of the popular 'hits' of the C list.

To be played affectionately as the performance direction tells us, this piece needs total liquidity of line, good chordal balance and well-organized legato pedalling. The expression is within a narrow range of dynamics, but within this the tone colours should be warm.

Fingering needs careful consideration to preserve the legato line of the melody, and pedalling will help to achieve a smooth delivery, too.

The rhythm could be swung to enhance the 'popular' flavour of the style. Examiners will accept it swung or straight, as long as the basic pulse is stable. There is added interest in the second half (from bar 25) when the melody is repeated an octave higher in the right hand. Here the left hand has an expressive counter-melody which should be shaped up to the A in bar 27, and projected through the texture, for variety.

Look out for the *meno mosso* at the end when winding down. The song needs long pedals to create a relaxed, almost haunting atmosphere.

C:6 Shostakovich *Gavotte*

An earlier age of powdered wigs and ornate costumes is evoked in this pastiche of a Baroque dance. Although written in 4/4, this light-hearted Gavotte calls for a sense of two-in-a-bar, to maintain the cheerful character (have *Tranquillo semplice* always in mind, though, so as not to rush the tempo). At first sight this may seem a long piece, but pupils will be pleased to note that there are many repetitions. The learning stage is made easier if the repeated material is pointed out and mastered in sections.

This piece would suit the pupil who has a good sense of keyboard geography and who can move over the keys with physical ease and freedom.

Both hands (but particularly the left) leap around over wide intervals, so encourage students to learn the piece from memory, in the interests of accuracy. Remember, however, that playing from memory is not a requirement for the exam.

Within this clearly stylized articulation, crotchets should in general be lightly lifted and dancing, giving a buoyant style. Chord shapes in the middle (minor) section need to be well formed in the hand, and lots of practice in covering the notes before playing them will help achieve precision in the performance. The dynamics focus on the softer end of the range, and accents need to be delicately articulated, without force or excessive weight, which would make them sound rather clumsy.

The final section returns to the opening theme, and the last spread chord gives a tongue-in-cheek ending with a coquettish smile.

GRADE 6

The big hurdle of Grade 5 Theory, Practical Musicianship or Grade 5 Jazz will be successfully over as work begins on Grade 6. The slightly different criteria for the higher grades, printed in *These Music Exams*, emphasize the need for the musical character, style and details to come across with conviction. Hopefully, by now the technical fluency will support these developing ideas, allowing more focus on expressive stylistic aspects.

A:1 John Loeillet *Corant*

The elegance and persuasive sequences of this dance are hard to resist. It is sure to be a winner.

Although the corant is a lively dance, the texture of the left hand with its held notes and overlapping parts suggests that the composer was looking for sonority and a fairly legato sound. In order to achieve this, it must feel as though the fingers of the left hand are clinging to the keys through each bar, lifting the hand gracefully at the third beat and dropping again into the first beat of the next bar. Against this background the quavers flow expressively, the rise and fall of the melody dictating the dynamic shading.

Descending sequences always inspire a special response in the listener, and this piece has many, the first beginning in the second half of bar 4. It would be a good idea to ask your pupil to identify all the others, including one that rises rather than descends. The harmony makes considerable use of another significant Baroque feature, the 'cycle of fifths', which is usually heard accompanying the sequences.

The legato nature of the music has been mentioned already, but there are places where detached notes will provide contrast. The left-hand crotchets (from bar 60) could be detached except for first beats, where slurs will give them weight and emphasize their harmonic significance. Slurs can also be employed to highlight that special rhythmic device, the hemiola, which occurs in the approach bars to all the main cadences in this piece. For instance, in bars 11–12 slur the crotchets in pairs so that three minim beats are heard across the two bars. This same device can be found at bars 28–9 and 68–9 but rather less obviously at 45–6 and 58–9.

Don't be afraid of the ornamentation – there are only two tricky passages and, if necessary, these can be slightly simplified. From bar 20 (and again in the second half) the trills on third beats could be reduced to a simple turn of four notes without destroying the desired effect, and trills over quavers (bars 29, 59 and 69) played as acciaccaturas. Just a little patience will be amply rewarded by this expressive piece.

A:2 Arne *Andante*

This beautiful cantilena-style andante is full of longing and regret; it tugs at the heartstrings. It will appeal to those with a romantic soul who enjoy music from a period when the harpsichord was still in vogue.

The melody requires a flowing legato line with only the octave-leaping quavers being slightly detached and marked; your pupil should guard against holding the second quaver longer than the first, though. The left hand's part is mainly a supportive one, but there are some contrapuntal passages that deserve special attention. The tenor voice of the opening bars (and similar) should sing warmly above the descending chromatic bass line. Practising these passages on their own, lightly detaching the quavers in the bass, will allow the suspensions to be heard singing clearly above.

Ornaments and rhythm also require careful thought. The persistent triplets are the clue to both, for it was customary to loosen dotted-note figures and upbeats so that they matched the prevailing rhythm. Do not let the richness of the ornamentation cause alarm. The annotated realizations suggested by the editor give clear guidance, and with a little patience they will soon be flowing easily within the beat, enhancing the melody and raising the emotional impact of the music. On the harpsichord it is relatively easy to play the *pralltriller* or short trill over semiquavers (see bar 3), but the heavier keys of the modern piano make this difficult. It is simpler just to play what is in effect an acciaccatura, as is indicated above the trill sign. However, all ornaments should be played gently in this piece so as not to disturb the mood.

Look out for those moments when emotional intensity is heightened by the use of harmonic rhetoric. In bar 5, for instance, the pain expressed by a diminished 7th chord is then soothed with a tender Neapolitan chord (fourth beat), and in bar 20 a dramatic climax is built by means of chromaticism. As far as tempo is concerned, it would be helpful to think in quaver units until notes and rhythm are safe, but in performance feel the crotchet pulse carrying it along. A wide dynamic range should be avoided, the melodic shapes and the harmony alone suggesting nuances and contrasts in colour. Above all, enjoy!

A:3 J. L. Dussek *Allegro*

This is a good choice for the pupil who likes to tackle something substantial. There is a sturdiness and panache about the writing that brings to mind the early compositions of Beethoven – another famous piano virtuoso, who was just ten years younger than Dussek.

However, be aware that the dynamic level is often quiet – it even begins *piano* – and the accompaniments need always to be softer than the melodies. A common mistake is to overpower the thematic material, especially in loud passages or when making a crescendo. The Alberti basses will require a relaxed hand, and in bar 1 (and similar) pupils should notice that the notes change on the fourth beat – it would be easy to continue playing the same chord throughout the bar. Sufficient space needs to be given to the long rest and pause in bar 18, so that the second subject can make a really dramatic entrance in the next bar, and, in bar 41, pupils may need reminding that the left hand is still in the treble clef.

The left-hand passage from bar 63, where minims have to be sustained over steadily moving quavers, may prove tricky. It could be turned into a useful exercise for finger independence.

Where a bright attack is needed, quavers are best played staccato (e.g. the right hand in bars 1, 20 and 23), but the accompaniment at bar 19 and the cantabile passage from bar 43 should be legato. Pedal would help to add a bloom to this expressive theme, and in bars 19 and 21 it will give sonority to the *fortissimo* attack on the high notes. Elsewhere, pedal could be used to sustain longer chords and to fill out the climax of the final bars, but care should be taken not to cover rests or to blur the detail.

Dynamic marks are given generously and, if observed, will bring colour and contrast to the performance. The *rinforzando* (bar 73) is within a quiet context, so it just needs an accent rather like a whispered exclamation. From this subdued passage the coda emerges, and it would be exciting to begin a crescendo in bar 76, urging the music onwards to its triumphant conclusion.

A:4 C. P. E. Bach *Solo per il Cembalo in E flat*

This is a piece for the pupil who enjoys music with rhythmic energy and harmonic colour. As a keyboard virtuoso, C. P. E. Bach was greatly admired for his playing of the clavichord, an instrument capable of subtle dynamic shading and even vibrato (*bebung*). On the piano we cannot produce vibrato, but we can employ any amount of dynamic contrasts.

The piece starts boldly, but beginning too fast brings the danger of tripping up over the triplets that lie ahead (how appropriately they are named!). It would be stylistically correct to begin *forte*, but at bar 10 lighten the touch a little so that the triplets can ripple along easily. Dynamics will be suggested not only by the texture but also by the key changes and harmonic colouring. For instance, a *subito piano* in bar 16 followed by a crescendo will highlight the appearance of a special interrupted cadence involving a diminished 7th chord instead of the usual submediant.

When the same device is employed again, at bar 58, there is not quite the same element of surprise, and as the end is in sight it would be better not to drop the volume so much.

The second half contains further adventures, and the passage in C minor, beginning at bar 27, needs a gentle, persuasive tone followed by a gradual crescendo towards the dramatic phrases in G minor (bar 35). Then there is scope for an echo effect at bar 39, when a phrase containing more vivid diminished 7th chords is repeated.

Lightly detached quavers in the left hand will keep the texture buoyant, and provide a background to the more varied articulation of the right.

The ornamentation in this piece is not complicated. Use the short trill (*pralltriller*) that consists of four notes beginning on the upper note, except in bars 15, 19, 57 and 61. Here the slurs show that trills should be placed slightly *after* the beat and that they consist of only three notes starting on the principal note. The dotted-note figures in bars 25 and 57 must be really snappy, and the many syncopated rhythms that are such a feature of this engaging piece should be relished.

A:5 Telemann *Fuga prima in G minor*

For understanding the character of this vivacious piece, it might be useful for students to listen to a recording of a Baroque concerto grosso for strings. Typical of Telemann's keyboard writing, this piece blends two-part fugal passages with episodes of bravura and decorative figuration that conjure up the sound of violins and cellos.

The articulation is uncomplicated, especially if your student imagines the effect of detached bowing for the quavers and rather longer bows for the crotchets and tied notes. In keyboard terms, fingers should be gently curved so that fingertips can produce a bright, crisp attack. Monitor closely the semiquavers that follow tied quavers in bars 4 and 7; these need to be precise, and the slightest delay or heaviness on the first note will cause a hitch and co-ordination could suffer. These flowing semiquaver figures also contain meaningful intervals (falling 7ths and rising 6ths) that can be lightly pointed.

It would be appropriate to begin the *Fuga* with an unforced *forte* tone, but notice that there is a natural rise and fall to the shape of the subject that not only gives it a sense of forward movement but conveniently allows it to make way for the answering phrase each time. Dynamics will be a matter of choice and for discussion with your pupil. However, it is worth noting that where the music either ascends or descends in sequences, terraced dynamics could be employed to highlight the shape and direction of these phrases. A definite drive will be felt towards a climax in bars 23 and 24, and the crotchet rest should have a really dramatic impact before the powerful restatement of the subject, now in unison and in the home key. A slight pulling back of the tempo would be effective in the last bar, where the 'strings' are heard once more in unison.

There is no tempo marking, but everything in the score points to this being an *allegro* movement. Once the notes are safely under the fingers, the piece will prove exciting and rewarding to play.

A:6 Vanhal *Allegro*

Brightness and lightness are words to remember as your pupil prepares this delightfully carefree movement. The piece is musically uncomplicated in both structure and texture; the major–minor–major ternary form and repetition of figures offer plenty of scope for contrasts of mood and colour.

Technically, however, the music is not all plain sailing. It requires equal agility in both hands because much of the material is tossed back and forth between them. Performances are frequently marred by a less than efficient left hand, so give a little extra time to ensure that the hands really do match each other in matters of articulation and dexterity. The suggested metronome speed of dotted crotchet = 92 seems a little fast; you may want to try *c*.80–84.

Strong accents are out of place here, and it is best to avoid emphasizing every beat. Much of the music wants to dance along as one-in-a-bar, giving it buoyancy and forward movement. If your pupil has difficulty articulating the left-hand semiquavers in bar 4, try practising the group first by stopping on the fourth finger until that feels easy, and then adding the final note. Only if this fails to produce a crisp, even attack might a different fingering be tried.

In the middle section, a smoother, more expressive treatment of the melody would be effective, but the accompanying chords with repeated notes (bars 2 and 3 after the change into A minor) sound more natural if they are slightly detached – similarly when the hands swap roles two bars later. Five bars before the return to A major, the recommended edition suggests playing octaves in the right hand – a typical means of thickening the texture at a climax in keyboard music of this period – but if they are played, watch that the *forte* is not overdone.

The pedal could be employed to sustain chords or add fullness, but use it sparingly so that the musical detail and rests are not obscured. Vanhal is a composer whose music is rarely heard, but this is a piece that will be enjoyed by performer and listener alike.

B:1 Bridge *Impromptu*

This piece conjures up a magical dreamscape, infused with languor and distant exoticism. It will suit the pupil who has a sense of 'make-believe' and a keen sensitivity to sonority.

One of the piece's most striking features is the very long pedal markings. Don't be afraid to follow these – they do work and, without the resonance they create, the piece will be less able to cast its spell. The only place where a modification may work is in bar 3, where a half-pedal may just clear the air in a very resonant acoustic. However, the piece does have clear harmonic patterns, so in order to avoid muddling these it is equally important to change the pedal where marked. Generally, the pedalling follows the phrasing rather than the bar lines.

Although highly evocative, the piece calls for only subtle rubato over and above the tempo modifications already marked. (The ending, for example, has an in-built ritardando.) From bar 27 on careful counting will be necessary to realize the expansiveness of the music: any pushing on through fear of 'hanging around' will detract from the atmosphere. The suggested metronome mark will generate exactly the right amount of gentle forward movement, which should have an easy flexibility within it, showing an awareness of the changing phrase lengths. Literally breathing in time with the phrases may help to develop the necessary ebb and flow.

The piece needs the proverbial velvet touch, never rising above a serene *mezzo-forte* and taking in many gradations below this level. Use of the *una corda* will enhance bars 23–5 and from bar 40 to the end. Within this overall dynamic level, the examiner needs to hear a gentle projection of the melodic fragments, such as those in the right hand in bars 1–3 (and in the left in bars 21–3). Careful attention to balance is necessary for the flowing quaver figures to be suitably accompanimental.

If your pupil has not yet explored the wonders of musical impressionism, here is an excellent introduction. It can also be practised late at night without disturbing anyone!

B:2 Grieg *Einsamer Wanderer*

The idea of the individual alone with nature is one that has appealed to romantic temperaments from Schubert to Vaughan Williams. Grieg's rather contemplative piano miniature represents, perhaps, a more thoughtful wanderer, moving through the Norwegian countryside.

There is certainly no march-like tread, and a sense of whimsical nostalgia pervades much of the writing. This needs to be conveyed via a seamless legato within phrases, for which a very slight overlap of one note with the next may be a helpful image. Phrases should, ideally, be realized by touch and nuance rather than by gaps in sound, however brief.

Technically, the biggest challenge is probably presented by the parallel 6ths in bars 3 and 7. An alternative to the printed (though excellent) fingering is to effect the change of hand position after the dotted quaver and then finger the upper line with 3-4-5 and the lower with 1-1-2. The lower line in the second of these passages (bar 7) might be more comfortable if played 1-1-1. This is the more awkward of the two passages (whichever fingering you adopt), but note that pedalling throughout the entire dotted-crotchet beat is practically unavoidable.

As with much nineteenth-century music, pedal needs to be employed over and above where specifically marked, discreetly in the opening measures and mainly to ensure that repeated notes sound legato. The pedal is used more texturally in bars 9 and 11, where half-bar pedalling will enhance the rather astringent harmonic colour. Where Grieg seems to want the resonance to cover rests, make sure these are felt, if not heard.

The metronome mark implies a quite steady *allegretto*. But even a slightly slower tempo will ensure that our traveller does not become too much of a dawdler! The crescendo and 'stretto' of bar 14 can be analogously applied to bar 25, and each *poco ritard.* will be most effective if it concludes below tempo, thereby allowing the *a tempo* to tell. Accents need to be understood in context, as if gently introducing the phrase shapes, and the dynamic level should be intimate, allowing for a substantial rise to the more impassioned moments at bars 14–16 and 25–7.

There is a lot to think about in this brief span of 30 bars, but also a lot to enjoy!

B:3 Granados *Vals poético No. 5*

There must be few of us who can resist the allure of a lilting waltz rhythm, and here is one that conveys the glamour and romance of the genre.

To project this style, it is important that the left hand defines a feeling of one-in-a-bar, and the suggested metronome mark, which is for the whole bar, will aid this. Generally, there needs to be a slight lean into the downbeat of the left hand, as if launching the rest of the bar. This approach may need modifying from bar 19, because it could detract from the longer phrases. Here, it can help to 'ease in' the right-hand quavers and aim for the middle of the phrase. A useful practice would be to take, say, a scale of B flat major and play it in the right hand for the equivalent of four bars of 3/4, gradually increasing the dynamic into the third bar, then decreasing it to the end.

Note how the right-hand's accents help to give the piece character. There is a little game here, creating 2/4 in the right over 3/4 in the left, but this must be achieved subtly – over-accentuation will rob the music of its elegance. The marked ritardandos (or rallentandos) need to be apparent but not to the extent that the tempo reaches a near standstill. The semiquavers in bars 4, 8, 11 and so on can be delayed by a hair's breadth, as if 'belonging' to the ensuing dotted minims, as long as the left-hand beat is maintained.

The tone should be full-bodied, especially in the first half, but never hefty. Even the more delicate second half needs clear right-hand projection with a feeling, always, of reaching the key bed. Too 'feathery' a sound will struggle to create a sense of line. In the first part, pedalling by the bar will mostly work very well, but from bar 19 it will probably be more effective if cleared for the third beat.

Although a waltz, this piece has a poetic aspect. The examiner should be able to recognize the dance in question but not necessarily be able to dance to it…

B:4 Chopin *Prelude in B minor*

Thanks to a rich legacy of great recordings of the Chopin Preludes, we can appreciate the many different aspects of these masterpieces. Listening to a few such performances will promote discussion, and may help your pupil arrive at his or her own interpretation.

Such a richly expressive piece invites comparisons with other media and, as the texture nowhere exceeds four parts, it might be helpful to imagine a string quartet in which the cello bares its soul, only once entering into dialogue with the first violin in bars 6 to 8. Indeed, if feasible, listening to the bass line played on the cello (all but one bar is within the instrument's range) could stimulate thoughts about phrasing and dynamics.

Clearly the left hand needs maximum projection, using a deep, firm touch, while a shallower right-hand movement should gently emphasize the first of the duplets, with a subtle down-up motion. The *sotto voce* probably applies more to the right hand than to the left, where a response to the rise and fall of the phrases is called for. Try thinking of the opening semiquaver B as *pianissimo*, which rapidly rises to a healthy *mezzo-piano* for the middle of the phrase before sinking back down. It is effective to maintain a slightly louder level through bars 6 to 8, in order to reflect the harmonic intensity of the passage.

The textures should be richly pedalled, with at least one change per beat being generally a desirable minimum – although there are places where resonance can last through the bar, as at bars 4 and 12. With its increased harmonic rhythm, however, bar 8 will need to be accommodated by half-beat changes.

There is, of course, a range of acceptable tempi for this piece. The expression *assai*, however, is more likely to mean 'enough' rather than its acquired meaning of 'very'; too slow and the music could drag and lose its coherence. Try avoiding, also, excessive rubato, though you may like to 'place' the G major harmonies at bars 5 and 11, and certainly some gesture is desirable in response to the wonderful shock of the interrupted cadence at bar 18. A slight ritardando through the last few bars could help bring the music to a peaceful conclusion.

B:5 Heller *Song without Words*

In the nineteenth century, nature was often a source of inspiration for musicians, and the gently flowing quaver motion here could suggest a scene by a river. The 'song' might be one in which the first speaker is talking in subdued, connected phrases (bars 1–16 and so on); the second in more assertive, disjointed phrases (as in bars 17 and 18, 21 and 22); while the third, at a lower pitch, offers occasional reflections (e.g. bars 8, 27, 31–2).

Contrasting characterization of these elements is necessary whatever the interpretation and, to achieve a cantabile effect for the first, a sense of the arm weight leaning into the outer fingers of the right hand is needed. Larger hands may like to take the tenor B in bars 1, 3, 31 and 33 with the right hand, thereby removing the necessity for the left-hand leap. The fingering for the upper part would then have to be 4/2, 5/3, 4/2 on each occasion. Projection of the second melodic idea is more straightforward, but it should not be too harsh. The engaging little contributions to the bass, particularly those between bars 31 and 34, although marked *pianissimo*, may need a little help, otherwise their role will be lost under the upper sonorities.

The dynamic level at bar 41 should not be too thunderous – perhaps think of '*f*' as standing for 'full' rather than *forte* – although do enjoy the texture of the left-hand octaves, which should be dropped into rather than hit. Earlier, a slight 'comma' before the *pianissimo* in bar 19 will help to define this sudden change in dynamic, which could easily be overshadowed by the tail of the preceding *mezzo-forte*.

Pedal is needed throughout the music, over and above the printed markings (thus avoiding ungainly non-legato intrusions). For example, bars 5, 13 and similar will benefit from pedalling by the beat, as will bars 17 and 18. Also, the 3rds that open bars 1, 3, 9, 11 and so on will be aided by this touch of extra resonance. However, you will probably feel the need for an additional change in bar 14, to avoid blurring tonic and dominant harmonies together – this is not a charming effect, and charm is of the essence here.

B:6 Schütt *In the Garden (Im Garten)*

One can imagine the composer watching children at play in a garden and responding with this evocation of innocent pleasures. Imaginative players will enjoy the melodic and harmonic content of this music with its unexpected twists and changes of key.

Technically, perhaps the biggest challenge is presented by the left-hand leaps which occur throughout the piece. To aid accuracy, it is useful to glance at the keyboard immediately prior to the execution of these leaps while keeping a mental note of one's place on the page. Eye rather than head movement is helpful in this regard. Once this is mastered, it is important that the balance should favour the right hand, since this carries the melodic interest throughout. Ornaments do not need to be played too quickly and should sound like an integral feature of the melody, particularly if *con grazia* is to be realized.

Grace and charm are key to the music's character. This piece is essentially a waltz, requiring a gentle momentum and an awareness of the role of downbeats in creating the necessary lilt. Rigidity would be out of character, and tasteful rubato can be helpfully applied in places such as bars 8 and 16. The marked pedal changes work very well, but don't be afraid to experiment: for example, depending on the piano and the acoustic, you may feel the need to change on the third beats of bars 19 and 24, although generally the E flat major section needs a warmer sound and plenty of upper-note projection. *Una corda* can certainly be applied during the last two bars, but this colour is not really appropriate for any extended passage elsewhere in the piece.

Rests such as in bars 3 and 12 are important features, but any suggestion of snatching at the preceding staccato quavers should be discouraged. Indeed, all staccatos should be kept light and non-percussive if the grace of the musical picture is to be conveyed. Examiners will particularly enjoy a performance that can explore subtleties at the lower end of the dynamic spectrum.

C:1 Brian Bonsor *Feelin' Good*

There is a happy-go-lucky personality to this very attractive and cheerful jazz number. It has all the joie de vivre of a Frank Sinatra film, and needs confidence and good technique.

The instruction 'light and very rhythmic' should be taken to heart, especially for the outer sections. A breezy tempo is called for, though the metronome marking seems a touch frantic. The piece could certainly be played as steady as crotchet = 138 if the right touch is used and the performance kept sprightly, with a typical jazz emphasis on the final swung semiquaver in the crotchet beat.

A slightly detached touch in the right hand (not too legato) will help give the piece energy and rhythmic clarity. Keeping the chords precise yet quiet will also aid clarity, as well as avoid any muddiness.

In the outer sections a firm and absolutely exact sense of pulse is required, so to this end working with a pre-recorded drumbeat on an electric piano (or computer) is to be recommended. If this is not possible, encourage tapping something out on the piano top – anything to instil a really secure groove and swing feel.

The middle section (from bar 17), however, can have more pliancy and time. Here little details can make a big difference. The beginning of the triplet run in bar 20, for instance, could be kept right out of the way of the texture, coming through at the end of the bar to lead onto the next phrase. All the right-hand chords, meanwhile, need a focus to the top notes to present a confident sense of line, and the changing bar lengths should be so internalized that they sound perfectly natural and comfortable.

Throughout the piece take careful note of the pedal markings, which are excellent if taken literally. Where *secco* is called for, keep the sound dry but not harsh. The bass notes of the spread left-hand chords in bar 14 must be caught by the pedal and sustained.

The final two bars are a joy to play. A feature should be made of the light laughing run and the cheeky ending, with lots of time taken here.

C:2 Norman Dello Joio *Prayer of the Matador*

As preparation for this piece, you could discuss with your pupil what exactly the matador's prayer might be. Have also a range of Spanish music to discuss, from Soler through Granados to Dello Joio. The habanera from Bizet's *Carmen* or Ravel's *Pièce en forme de habanera* would be a good introduction.

The subtlety and effectiveness of the performance will come from an idiomatic and discreetly controlled opening rhythm (just fractionally delaying the semiquaver), and a bolder, well-shaped inner line, lingering just a little on the B♭ in bar 2.

The melody, or prayer, needs to be free and heartfelt, meandering its way over the top of the habanera rhythm, with just the occasional characteristic hesitation before the triplet figure (e.g. in bar 7).

Foremost among all musical considerations should be an improvisatory feel, with subtle shading through dynamics. Repeated notes should always have a musical shape, the melody uninterrupted by the accompaniment. Careful attention needs to be given also to the sustained notes, by listening through the texture and adjusting the balance so that the held note moves on without an accent. The repeated Es, which provide the rhythm, should always be soft and in the background, providing no more than a gentle pulse.

Carefully considered fingering is essential for control, and substitution will play a role in this at times. The marked fingerings work well.

Throughout the piece a warm haze of pedal, carefully and judiciously used, will provide the right atmosphere. Pedalling each bar where the right hand has the melody or on each crotchet beat when it's the left hand's turn should provide a starting point.

The range of dynamics in this piece is not huge; even the *forte* in bar 19 needs to be judged carefully as it could easily become boisterous. (It is more an emotional plea than a burst of anger.)

At no stage should the performance sound hurried or restless. Players should opt for expressiveness, allowing the prayer the full breadth and weight of meaning to convey the most personal and sincere sentiment.

C:3 A. Tcherepnin *Bagatelle No. 9*

This light and comic miniature has hints of melancholy, and is reminiscent of a small clockwork toy performing, rather disjointedly, the movements of a slightly grotesque dance.

It is effectively a study in light staccato and as such is invaluable as well as appealing. The secret is to feel totally at home with a firm yet quick staccato close to the keys, the notes controlled yet short. For this, a well-rounded hand is required, with the very end of the finger (just behind the nail) contacting the key, using just the corner (not the whole) of the thumb. With this, a quick bounce, plenty of hand weight and just a little action of the finger is possible, producing a really short, light yet vibrant staccato. If in doubt, try this on a tabletop and listen to the sound produced; a clear and short 'tap' should be heard, not a padded 'thud'.

Once the technique is mastered, the piece will almost play itself from the musical point of view. There are a few tricky corners (e.g. in bars 4 and 43), and there is need for occasional pedal and some authoritative shaping of the melody. Too much of anything, however, will destroy the simplicity. It is the fluency and ease that will draw out the character, and this can only be achieved with the most conscientious preparation of fingering and plenty of separate practice of hands.

Avoid too fast a tempo. A speed that allows sensitivity and control of touch is essential, and the player can certainly be flexible with the pulse around one or two of the trickier corners – but only if this can be done with musical conviction. What is undoubtedly a tricky piece will need to sound as if it has the simplicity of a nursery rhyme – almost casually 'tossed aside'.

C:4 Richard Rodney Bennett *Eight maids a-milking*

This witty and merrily 'pastoral' piece has eight maids in the title but only seven beats in the bar. The piece is exciting and fun to play but not without a few awkward moments technically. The time signature itself shouldn't pose too many problems, but it would be worth spending some time clapping through the rhythmic phrases, before singing and then playing them. Being able to see and hear the musical patterns amid the quavers will help the musical direction, memory and interpretation.

Co-ordination between the hands will need monitoring. The left hand will instinctively want to play too late, or too early, and undoubtedly the easiest solution to this is to work in small sections – unrhythmically at first, if necessary, just asking the hands to play notes at the appropriate time. The sections can then be played in time, and speeded up.

Contrast and shading in dynamics are needed to draw out the character of the piece. The first three two-bar phrases, for instance, all need a sense of purpose: the first moves towards the main, minim chord, but the second builds beyond this and towards bars 5 and 6. The middle section, marked legato, needs a warmer tone, and some judicious pedalling with a gentle rise and fall in dynamics.

The staccato of the outer sections requires a firmness of touch close to the key surface; plenty of energy in the fingers needs to be backed up by a confident wrist staccato. The right-hand chords should be used as a 'springboard' for the subsequent quavers, giving a little emphasis to the three-plus-four feel.

The ending is virtuosic and exciting – perhaps cows are mistaken for bulls here – and to enhance this, the *mezzo-forte* in bar 33 could benefit from being softer, exaggerated to even *piano*. The crescendo then has real impact, and the piece can finish with aplomb.

C:5 Christopher Norton *Lavender's Kind of Blue*

This is surely a piece for those in their second childhood as much as for those in their first, and it may well appeal even more to adults (who will definitely see or hear the joke). A clever and attractive slant on the nursery rhyme, this is a joy to play as it lies so comfortably under the fingers.

With its introduction, two verses and coda, the structure is very clear. The melody is almost too obvious, since at first it's in a sumptuous tenor and is then shared between high and low registers.

The whole piece needs an improvisatory, bluesy rubato, and a spontaneity – paradoxically – that only comes with complete familiarity with the notes and the technical challenges. Plenty of dynamic shape and pliancy is required during the opening phrases, perhaps making a ritenuto into bar 4 and again into the first verse in bar 8.

The semiquavers should be thoroughly rehearsed into the fingers. They need to weave their way with ease around the melody, responding to any time taken through the longer notes and helping the listener to follow the rubato. Clearly defined fingering and a relaxed technique, particularly in the wrist and hand, will help achieve a subtlety of light and shade. The melody should have a firm tone projected well to the front of the texture by using plenty of weight behind strong fingers.

Absolute control of the semiquavers is needed, again, in the second half, where the tune is heard over and under them. Despite the *forte* marking, as accompaniment their dynamic should be down to allow the melody through. The dotted-minim chords, meanwhile, are impossible to hold without plenty of pedal.

Technically, this same passage may be a little dangerous. Moving the left hand across the right and controlling the sound in both hands is not easy; at first, I would spend time just practising the melodic phrases over a stationary right hand resting gently on the key surface. This will help the 'feel' of using more weight and producing a bolder tone in the left hand without it affecting the right-hand semiquavers.

The pedal should be used freely and warmly, but some planning is needed to avoid adjacent and conflicting harmonies. In the end, on a different piano and in a different room, more or less pedal may be needed, so the student must adjust as the sound dictates, listening carefully.

A misty and spacious 'Lavender's Blue' in the last few bars maintains the atmosphere to the end.

C:6 Karen Tanaka *Lavender Field*

Pupils who have been to Normandy or western France will have little trouble appreciating the headiness and atmosphere of these lavender fields. This is a piece full of scented harmonies, with gently drifting quavers; it needs plenty of repose and deep, gentle breaths.

The right hand wanders carefree across the keys, so should not be too conspicuous: use a light arm and gentle, caressing, slightly flattened fingers for the sound. I would be tempted at first to practise the quavers with exaggerated dynamics and rubato, later moderating this as musical ideas and possibilities emerge.

The whole piece requires a pedalled 'heat-haze', with pedalling at appropriate moments to enhance the changing harmonies, without ever intruding. Begin the piece with the damper pedal already depressed and the fingers on the key surface. The tempo should then be eased in gradually and gently, the notes speaking initially with a little weight but then immediately without that weight, so that the fingers just keep the harmony sounding. This touch is very light.

Pedal changes should be after the note concerned but before its release. Take a little time at first around the difficult changes, rather than risk losing a note or blurring conflicting harmonies.

The melody should sing through confidently and be the guiding influence on the rubato. Longer notes need particular attention, with the pupil listening to ensure that sufficient tone sustains them throughout their whole length, and that they project over the accompaniment.

The dynamics throughout deserve thorough exploration, and the captivating sonority of the harmonies in the last bars should be relished. The pedal should not be lifted too abruptly at the end. Instead, suggest damping the sound gently to maintain the atmosphere right up to the closing silence.

GRADE 7

The final grades should be equally rewarding to teachers, pupils and parents, whose involvement in the exams should be bearing fruit. The playing usually sounds quite accomplished even at a pass level, while merit and distinction categories will acknowledge musical and polished performances of real artistic quality. The highest marks most frequently go to candidates choosing pieces within their own technical comfort zone, so that expressive details and communication can lift the music off the page.

A:1 Handel *Allegro*

It can be daunting for a student to see pages of semiquavers. Once the violinistic style of this piece is explained, however, and some background to the instrumental *sonata da chiesa* is given, a nimble-fingered player will be excited by the challenge.

The suggested metronome mark makes for a lively pace, and this momentum should be maintained. This can prove difficult if the right hand tires, so from the outset promote rotary movement in the wrist, to help prevent physical tension. This side-to-side rocking technique can be mastered by making an exaggerated movement at slow tempo and keeping the fingers' top joints firm and supported. As the notes become familiar and the speed is increased, the wrist movement should become smaller, almost down to a little nudge, with the strength in the fingers producing the brilliance in the sound.

The points of rest, though short, are important. They should be built into the choreography of the hand movements, the hand being lifted to relieve any tension that may occur. This movement not only encourages technical ease in the flow of the line but also provides musical punctuation.

The articulation in the right hand should be light but firm, with the first notes of the semiquaver groups perhaps highlighted to give melodic definition (in bars 11 and 12, and so on). Heavy accentuation should be avoided at all costs. The left hand will be effective if lightly detached throughout.

Some unexpected leaps of wide intervals in the right hand (bars 5, 10, 13 and so on) might catch the player by surprise; lots of practice judging these leaps, covering the notes carefully in slow motion, will help avoid accidents in performance. Particular care should be taken at bars 29 and 30 when the rising sequence has two intervals of a 6th followed by a third interval of a 9th. Establishing the fingering in both parts is essential for accuracy and smoothness of delivery; it also helps to highlight familiar scale patterns, as in bars 13 and 33.

The blank canvas here means that you and your pupil can create a scheme of dynamics to match the contours of the writing. Consider some echo-phrasing to give an antiphonal effect (e.g. in bars 11 and 12), and devise a plan to enhance the harmonic structure.

A:2 J. W. Hässler *Presto*

At first sight this piece may seem relatively easy for Grade 7, but the ornamentation and the *presto* indication – demanding lively fingerwork and clarity of touch – make this more challenging. The choice of tempo will make or break this performance, so this is a piece in which metronome practice will help prevent notes running away with themselves. Starting with scale passages in C major can lead to some skidding on the white notes, especially by players who tend to race when under pressure. Even when the piece is well known to your pupil, continual 'laundering' – in other words, slow practice, separate-hand practice, and metronome work (starting slowly and working up to the recommended mark) – will help keep it clean and tidy.

Ornamentation is often a stumbling-block. Try to have the trills and mordents integrated into the texture from the early stages of learning; adding them later can cause rather lumpy lines. Remember that the ornaments are there to be decorative, not destructive, and that examiners are always delighted to hear neat embellishments.

A strong sense of rhythm is needed; your pupil should think of a swinging two-in-a-bar but remember to count the rests precisely (in bars 18, 20, 22 and so on), to enhance the regular lilt. These bars, in addition, can present co-ordination problems, as the player must tuck in the left-hand repeated notes with ease. Where the right hand has *staccatissimo* markings, suggest a discreet accent on the main beats, to help keep the hands under control and to maintain rhythmic buoyancy. In similar bars in the second section (bars 57 to 64), the rests are filled in with semiquavers and what follows are two bars in which the right hand crosses over the left. This right-hand change into the bass clef may be missed by some students.

As the texture must remain clear, the pedal should be employed only with the utmost discretion. Use it to glaze the sounds of the dotted crotchets in bars 28, 30, 50, 52, and also to join the sounds of the dotted minim to the dotted crotchet over the bar lines (bars 34–5, 37–8, 76–7, 79–80), putting the pedal down late in the first bar of these pairs to avoid smudging the left-hand semiquavers. Do guard against pedalling throughout; one of the most common faults heard by examiners is over-pedalling of pieces in Baroque and Classical styles. This sunny piece will bring much enjoyment to the examiners if the lightness of the style is well managed.

A:3 Mozart *Allemande*

One could easily mistake the composer of this stately Allemande, as it looks very much like Handel or Bach on the written page. Clearly influenced by these Baroque composers, this movement is very expressive and needs prudent separate-hand learning from the outset, in order for all the fingering to become second nature. This piece is not entirely suitable for students who find note-learning tricky and who invent their own (often illogical) fingering. It is a potential minefield for missed accidentals, ties, wrong notes and incorrectly held note-lengths. That said, the rewards of studying such a masterpiece would be very great: a sense of satisfaction comes with having learnt it 'hands together', and the flowing style is compelling.

In Mozart's music (as in Beethoven's) the key of C minor is associated with melancholy and a more darkly expressive side. With this feeling in mind, the dynamics (which are left to the performer) should be appropriately graded within a warm sound; never too bright in *forte*, but with a rise and fall to mark the phrasing. Also, care is needed to define the part-playing clearly – the left-hand semiquavers in broken-chord shapes, whether rising or falling (e.g. bars 1, 2, 5 and 6), may be overlooked by more right-handed players, to the extent that these fail to weave in beautifully with the top lines.

The piece is full of suspended lines which must be held fully for the harmony to be realized. A legato touch is appropriate, and many substitutions of fingers as marked (bars 8, 10, 16, 21, 22, 26) are necessary to maintain the connection of the lines. Watch for the accidentals that are not so immediately obvious, such as in bar 4 where B♮s compete with a B♭.

A:4 J. S. Bach *Corrente*

There is something wonderfully joyful about Bach's writing in G major. This Corrente (the Italian variety of the Baroque 'running' dance which

87

follows the Allemande in the dance suite) demands fleeting fingerwork and excellent control and evenness of tone. The dangers of this kind of piece for the less experienced performer playing on an unfamiliar piano are known to us all – setting off at an ambitious pace, then either hurrying with the inevitable breakdown to follow or slowing down to accommodate the less technically secure passages. A one-in-a-bar feeling will help decide the tempo, and the left hand – in the first section – will provide the anchorage for the right hand's weaving line. The second half demands a flowing left hand and considerable work if both hands are to enjoy equal agility.

The ornaments should enhance the line and not be (as they so often become) stumbling blocks for the candidate. It would be helpful to incorporate them into the line from the beginning of the learning process. Careful attention to fingering (always important, especially so in contrapuntal music) should be encouraged from the outset to ensure note accuracy when exam nerves come into play.

Recommend a light touch to your students. The quavers could be detached or given some slurring for contrast (e.g. over the first two quavers in bars 1 and 3, left hand, and similarly in the right hand in bar 33). The semiquavers should also be light, yet with pointing in the line to make some melodic definition. For example, highlight the first, third and fifth semiquavers in rising broken-chord figures, such as in bar 2, and then the first semiquaver of bar 3.

A scheme of dynamics needs careful consideration, and guidance should be given to your students to achieve overall musical shape. Instances of *forte* must be bright and never heavyweight. Begin with one such *forte* to establish the character immediately. You may like to suggest a drop in level, down to *piano*, for the minor section at bar 37. A build-up to the end could begin at bar 49, and reach *forte* for the swirling broken-chord figures in both parts at bar 57 – in time for the triumphant close.

A:5 Beethoven *Allegro*

This movement from the early Sonata Op. 7 lies at the more difficult end of the spectrum for Grade 7. Fundamentally a Scherzo and Trio, the *allegro* marking implies a lively tempo, but with a graceful feel of one-in-a-bar. Control of the tempo is essential from the outset; it is easy to set off at a fast pace without considering the speed of the triplets in the *Minore* section. This can catch inexperienced players unawares, and they should be advised to think of those triplets before beginning the movement.

The Allegro should be played in a lyrical style and the melody in the top line should sing. The silences need to be measured, and rests given their full value, for the phrasing to make musical sense. At bar 25 point out the two-part imitation (led by the bass), which should be well projected, to build the crescendo as the musical line rises. Later, in bar 86, the tenor line has the melodic interest and needs careful voicing, the soprano answering at bar 90.

The dynamics should be carefully noted, especially the *ppp* at the end of the *Minore*: this marking is rare in Beethoven, so he clearly intends a special distant effect. Extra special care is needed in the playing of the *sforzandi* (in bars 16, 17 and 18). So often pupils treat these as thunderous accents, without consideration of the prevailing dynamic (*pianissimo* in bar 13); try to encourage a lighter, more pointed sound for these. Other *sforzandi* in the left hand, in bars 19, 21 and 80–84, need a warmer, more weighted touch to exaggerate the slurring.

The *Minore* poses a technical challenge from the point of view of hand co-ordination. Here the mood changes significantly. An even tone is needed in both hands, with sounds being sustained by the fingers (*sempre legato*) and also by judicious use of pedal – some quick changes are needed if smudges in the harmony are to be avoided. Much slow practice (without pedal, to begin with) will reap rewards later. There is an opportunity for the use of the *una corda* here; this would change the timbre and give it the darker sound quality that Beethoven indicates by his change of key and writing style. As always in exams, the da capo should be played.

This marvellous movement gives the student a chance to tackle a piece of major importance in the Classical repertoire. If its technical and musical demands are met, the performance will be rewarding for both performer and listener.

A:6 Haydn *Moderato*

The scene is set for an elegant, moderately-paced first movement, which needs buoyancy in the rhythm to be fully effective.

Adopting a flowing tempo at the start that will allow the sextuplet scales to sing and remain even is of paramount importance. Encourage your students to hear the speed of the semiquavers in their head before starting the piece, and thereby avoid scrambling the scales due to too fast a tempo. The rests at the end of bars 2 and 4 need to be given their full value – this is often a trap for young players, especially at the beginning of a piece when nerves are not fully under control. Here, again, they need to listen through the silences and to prepare mentally for the next phrase.

Ornamentation often causes anxiety among candidates, possibly because it's been incorporated after the initial learning of the outline. Work with your pupils to achieve well-integrated trills early on, thinking of the line as a vocal melody. Take care not to overlook the trills indicated by the small letter *t* at the ends of phrases (e.g. bar 12). In bar 9 the trill realization is particularly good; the same rhythm should be used for the trill in bar 52.

Aim to produce a beautiful cantabile sound, even in places of tricky co-ordination between the hands, such as bars 19 and 60. You may find it useful to isolate these bars, devising technical exercises from these patterns to achieve fluency and evenness. Heaviness in the touch should be avoided throughout, but extra special care is needed in *forte* passages, especially when there are left-hand octaves (such as in bar 5), which should not obscure the right-hand line. With wide jumps such as those in the right hand in bar 32, care is needed not just for note accuracy, but to ensure that the hand does not land on the top notes with a heavy accent. Consider matching the sounds of the end of one scale to the beginning of the next.

As always in Classical sonata movements, the pedal should be used with discretion, so as not to blur the harmony. However, legato pedalling might be appropriate in bars 36 to 41 (the end of the development section) to enhance the overall sonority, before the recapitulation.

This attractive, lyrical movement presents a delightful choice for musical pupils possessing nimble fingers and a good sense of rhythm.

B:1 Glière *Esquisse*

The mood of this lovely piece is one of nostalgia, but without the pangs of loss and regret so often heard in Russian music. The lyrical melody recalls only pleasant memories, despite the chromaticism of the counter-melodies and harmony that surround it.

The form of the piece is a simple but effective ABA, the middle section consisting of fragments of the theme and unexpected changes of key rather than new material. The tone, especially for the melodic lines, should be full and rich; but when it moves into the sharp keys (bars 11–13), encourage a brighter sound. Pedal will be required throughout – frequent changes on the quaver beat will prevent smudging of the harmony.

Balancing melody and accompaniment is quite easy, although the passage beginning in bar 13 needs care as interest shifts from the descending chromatic crotchets to the syncopated alto part in bars 15 and 16. When the melody is heard in the left hand it should be projected generously – imagine the warm, expressive tone of the cello – but when it makes its highest appearance (bars 17–20) the player must guard against forcing the tone. The piano can be coaxed into producing a beautiful bell-like sonority in this high register. The counter-melodies, while always subservient to the principal theme, do need a shape and life of their own. For instance, a very special moment can be created by making a crescendo in the alto line towards the Db in bar 24.

In Romantic music, grace notes are usually played before the beat. However, when grace notes appear with a chord (see bar 3) it is more satisfactory to play them *on* the beat. The only ones that may cause difficulty appear under the sustained crotchets in bars 13–15. As these crotchets descend, the hand may feel freer if the fifth finger is placed on the white keys and the fourth finger on the black.

One more fragment of the theme is heard in the closing bars, as though the composer cannot bear to let go of the past; the piece then fades away through a rising arpeggio figure. For groups that have extra notes in them – here we have ten in the time of eight – some pupils prefer to have a mathematical scheme, and it works well if the first six notes are thought of as triplets that slow down imperceptibly into the remaining four semiquavers. These final notes are marked with tenuto lines, and it is effective to play them by dropping the hand gently from above each key – more bells!

B:2 Grovlez *Chanson de l'escarpolette*

There is no doubt that having a story or picture in mind is a great aid to interpretation. Often we have only the title to go on, but in the case of Grovlez's delightful *L'almanach aux images* we are also given a poem for each piece. The one entitled 'Chanson de l'escarpolette' (Song of the Swing) describes children playing in the park, but there is an air of fantasy about the scene and it is the idealized children of Victorian storybooks who inhabit this world. In the poem, reference is made to the nineteenth-century artist Kate Greenaway and you can find a website showing some of her charming illustrations.

The swing is 'suspended by ropes of silk' and, with the pauses and rubato, one can clearly hear when it is being held back, and when it is released; when it is accelerating, and when it is slowing down again. The composer also likens the tempo and extravagant rhythmic movements to the Viennese waltz – altogether a vivid and colourful effect, in which syncopation plays a very important part.

Great care must be taken over accidentals because the 'dizziness' and excitement of swinging is portrayed by chromaticism and sudden changes of key; it is very easy to misread notes. The music is meticulously annotated, so every slur and staccato mark should be observed. Rests also play an important part, including the one at the very beginning that feels just like an intake of breath – a moment of delicious anticipation before the swing begins its descent.

Pedal will be needed, but on this occasion it is mainly the right-hand part that dictates where it should be applied. The broad gestures associated with the pauses need to be well sustained, but pedal must be changed on every beat along with the harmony, especially in the chromatic passages such as bars 6–8 and 14–16. Avoid pedalling on staccato notes except, perhaps, the cadence chords in bars 16–17. You might consider matching these to the cadence bars at the end where pedal is actually indicated. Here, too, the *una corda* pedal is required.

In bars 14–15 and 60–61 a more balanced and legato effect can be achieved if the lower notes of the right-hand chords are played by the left hand, but a reliable fingering will have to be established. The inner melody line in bars 20–23 needs projection, and in the following bars your pupil should enjoy a feeling of panache when playing the rising staccato 3rds all with the 2+4 fingers. So *now* your pupils know why they practised that scale in 3rds for Grade 6!

B:3 Schumann *Des Abends*

The haunting beauty of this portrayal of evening time is one of the treasures of the Romantic repertoire. This is music of the utmost tranquillity and tenderness, and it is worth remembering that at this time almost all of Schumann's compositions were inspired by his love for Clara Wieck, later to become his wife.

The melody falls and rises in a deep arc, like a slow pendulum, and throughout the piece Schumann links together two of his favourite motifs – a five-note descending theme originally written by Clara herself, and the curving figure that Robert invented around the musical letters of her name. In its 'unmasked' form it is **CBAG#A**, but here it appears in different keys. Neither the piquant dissonances nor the exquisitely subtle rhythm must be allowed to disturb the dreamy mood, and it may take some time and patience to achieve a smoothly flowing technique.

Schumann has contrived to intertwine two conflicting rhythms – the right hand sounds as though it is in triple time and the left in duple, but it is the left hand that underpins the rhythm while the melody drifts above in triplet quavers. At first it would be helpful to practise the melody line alone, leaving out the intervening semiquavers, so that a singing legato line can be developed. The fingering largely depends on placing the longer third and fourth fingers over the fifth finger when moving upwards, and passing the fifth under when moving downwards. (This system works best when the fifth finger is placed on white keys.) After attending to the melody line, your pupil can add the bass notes that occur on the first and second quaver beat of each bar (in the first bar these would be D♭ and A♭) so that the two against three can be heard in relief.

The idea of mingling or entwining is also seen in the texture of the music. The hands weave in and out, the thumbs crossing in patterns that are inspired by the piano itself. With only a few exceptions, the left thumb passes over the right in the flat keys but under the right when the key signature changes to sharps. Fluency will depend on knowing exactly where these thumb notes lie. The offbeat 'inner' melody lines are another of Schumann's devices (see bars 21–4), and these need to be clearly projected either using thumbs as indicated or, if preferred, a mix of thumbs and second fingers. As so much of the music is repeated, it would be effective sometimes to employ the *una corda* pedal to provide contrast, while the sustaining pedal blends the texture and supports the bass line.

B:4 Grieg *Butterfly*

This is sure to be a popular choice among pupils with nimble fingers and a love of descriptive pieces. Most editions have this piece spread over four pages, but do not let this be off-putting: quite a lot of the material is repeated.

How Grieg captured the fluttering of the butterfly's wings and its seemingly erratic flight from flower to flower is truly remarkable, and delicacy is the word to remember while playing this lovely piece. Accents are merely a method of drawing attention to the essential melody notes, and on those few higher phrases where *forte* is marked, it is brilliance rather than weight that is needed. The player should cultivate as many different shades of *piano* and *mezzo-piano* as possible, and make use of the *una corda* pedal where indicated. It is always immensely satisfying to play the very lowest note on the keyboard, as happens at the end of this piece, but notice that it is marked *pianissimo* – not the easiest thing to gauge on an unfamiliar piano when one is feeling nervous. No examiner will mind if a candidate tries out that key before commencing the performance.

Encourage your pupil to feel the natural rise and fall to the chromatic runs of the principal theme and to keep the semiquaver buoyant in the dotted-note figures. A feather-light left hand is essential; the pupil must be especially careful not to bump the thumb notes. There is also a danger of striking wrong notes with the thumb, and the subtle changes in harmony from bars 12 to 15 can sometimes lead to errors. Another trap is the full half-bar rest three bars before the end; careful counting is needed.

In most editions of the *Butterfly*, pedal markings are indicated but not always complete. The left hand's three-note broken-chord figures, for example, need touches of pedal to support them. The reliable use of pedal will add colour and sparkle to the playing and greatly assist freedom of movement across the keyboard. Rubato, too, is an important ingredient in the successful performance of any Romantic music, but bear in mind that there are already ritardandos and strettos in the score. The phrases should ebb and flow as naturally as possible without distorting the overall structure, and above all the picture of that butterfly must remain in mind.

B:5 Liszt *En Rêve*

With just a handful of notes, Liszt manages to create an ecstatic, dream-like piece that expresses great tenderness and tranquillity. It will suit the sensitive pupil who understands that it takes time and imagination to develop good tone control at the quietest dynamic levels.

The key of B major encourages the pianist to lay the fingers in a rather flat attitude over the keys. (It is no coincidence that Chopin made this the first scale that he taught new pupils, and his words 'easily, easily' are useful advice.) Awareness of the relaxed state of the arm is crucial as the gentle accompaniments are played, using just a little more weight for the melody lines that must sing sweetly above.

The principal melody appears first as a simple solo, its four-bar phrase played twice; later it returns in a slightly more elaborate form but still retaining its mood of the utmost calm. The additional notes must not disturb the gentle flow. The left hand should move as little as possible, keeping the fingers close to the key surface. In bar 10 it may be necessary for the player with a small stretch to release the E♯ minims and, from bar 21, glide as smoothly as possible over the wider intervals that begin to appear.

Pedalling is vital in this piece and the *pianissimo* tone together with the veiled sonorities means that some fairly long pedal effects can be attempted; there are places where the harmony does not change for several bars. *Una corda* pedal could be used throughout. It is marked at the beginning and again in bar 23, but there is no sign of it being released. Care should be taken not to hurry the passage from bar 13 – let it sound as though it is gently unwinding, without losing the underlying pulse.

A remarkable passage, starting in bar 29, where the music descends sequentially through keys from B to E as though drifting into sleep, leads to the exquisite moment when a nightingale begins to sing. The trill, at bar 35, will require plenty of practice, keeping the fingers as loose as possible, but now more curved in shape. The shifts from one trill to the next should be seamless, and it may be easier to use fingers 2 and 4 on the third trill, getting into position via the thumb on the first D♮ (bar 41). The spaced-out G♯ crotchets underneath *should* be played by the thumb of the right hand, but it is possible to cheat and roll the left hand over to reach them instead.

B:6 Skryabin *Prelude in G flat*

This is definitely one for the pupils who like to pick the shortest piece in the list (and with pressure of work these days, who can blame them?). However, be warned – the piece requires a mature pedal technique and the ability to etch out a melody from the top notes of chords. If chosen, though, the musical rewards will far outweigh the difficulties.

The melody line should first be played on its own so that it sings warmly and its shape is discovered. The ear will get to know this sound and it will then be easier to reproduce when playing with the full chords. Your student should notice that in bar 4 the third beat A♭, with its stem going up, is the melody note. The left hand's flowing counter-melody is next to be practised. Occasionally a hidden bass line of crotchet-minim pattern should emerge from the quavers. This is especially important in bars 15–18, where the lowest notes create a descending bass that will support the crescendo towards the approaching climax. Before finally filling in the harmony, the melody and counter-melody should be played together, adding some pedal now, and the player can begin to assess the balance.

Always be careful with accidentals in the early stages of learning; in this key they can easily be forgotten (for instance, do not miss the left hand's second F♭ in bar 20). There are quite a few tied notes about too, underlining the composer's intention of a very sustained sound. A redistribution of notes can occasionally be helpful, especially for the player with small hands. In bar 6 take the minim B♭ with the left hand and in the next bar the quaver C♭ with the right. Then in bar 24 if the D♭ dotted minim is played with the right thumb and the minim C♭ with the left thumb, the awkward stretches disappear.

Pedal will be required throughout, and though a certain amount of 'mixing' of sounds is inherent to the style, basic harmony changes should be clear. Close listening will reveal if muddiness makes an extra pedal change necessary. The use of *una corda* pedal will add colour in places, too. The ending is particularly beautiful, giving scope for some imaginative pedalling. By changing slightly later than usual, clear the C♭ from the harmony of bar 31 and then do not change the pedal until bar 33 so that the bell-like D♭ emerges gradually from the background...given enough tone it should still be heard as the final chord fades.

C:1 Bernstein *For Johnny Mehegan*

The rhythmic and colouristic elements of this piece make it an attractive choice, especially for the candidate who enjoys jazz idioms. With the more instrumentally minded pupil, you could imagine a big-band arrangement and have fun deciding where trombone, saxophone or trumpet sounds would be appropriate.

Since the rhythmic element is paramount, it would be helpful early on to count the whole piece carefully in quavers, making sure everything fits together. Remember that the silences are as crucial to the effect as the notes. Once the syncopations are mastered, it is important that the piece sounds natural rather than contrived. Playing with a synthesized keyboard rhythm or, better still, with a live rhythm-section, if available, will help in mastering the style. The metronome mark, though fast, yields exactly the right tempo for the feel of the piece. In a really skilful performance, the listener should want to tap his or her foot throughout the piece – but rest assured that the examiner will not do this!

The dynamic markings are very precise, almost suggesting a 'terraced' effect, and the examiner should be able to detect a clear difference between the six levels called for, as well as any 'hairpins' within these. There is an overall crescendo up to bars 16–17 and diminuendo to bar 23 (with the last three bars acting as a brief coda). A sense of general intensification to the climax followed by an 'unwinding' will reflect Bernstein's markings. The softest passages will benefit from *una corda*, especially the first few bars, which have an almost furtive character.

The marked articulation is equally precise and gives life to the rhythms. Most of the time, right and left hands correspond, but care needs to be taken where they go separate ways, as in bars 14–16; independence of hands will be needed for this passage to achieve its full effect. Although practising each hand separately will be suitable in the early stages of learning, it is perhaps more important to absorb the sense of how one hand relates to the other, slowly and systematically practising the simultaneous but contrasting actions.

The notes are not especially difficult to find; the main challenges lie elsewhere. Despite the jazzy language, a literal interpretation of the score will go some way to realizing its intentions – but it is that extra degree of panache and personality that will really make the music live.

C:2 Ravel *Valse*

The refined, pastel shades of this wistful little waltz will be well matched to the more inward-looking personality blessed with sensitive fingers. There is no overt romance in this dance, just a gentle nostalgia, as if looking backwards on happier days through the slightly distorting telescope of time.

The main problem in the early stages of learning will be to sort out the accidentals. Ravel's intentions seem very clear, so exactitude is essential. Thinking of enharmonic equivalents to some of the chords could be helpful. For example, the chord on the second quaver of both bars 19 and 20 translates as a second-inversion F major triad, and that on the second beat of both bars 25 and 26 equates to a triad of B flat major. Several of the inner lines of the treble-clef part move chromatically in parallel major 3rds, as in bars 10–11 and 13–14.

Ravel's metronome mark is just fast enough for a barely detectable lean into the first beats, to help preserve the waltz feel. The 32-bar span is symmetrically constructed and subdivides evenly into four-bar phrases. A hint of rubato at the ends of these phrases will ease in the next phrase, projecting a sense of structure, but guard against any sense of disconnection.

The dynamic level is mainly *piano* or below, only once rising to a level slightly above *mezzo-piano*. Some useful preparatory work might be to get your pupil to play a familiar but much simpler piece, condensing the dynamics to within Ravel's range, yet realizing the subtle differences.

Extensive use of *una corda* will be very helpful at the quietest end, producing exactly the right shades of colour. However, the melody will need to be projected and the upper-note cross-rhythms in bars 19–20 and 23–4 can be brought out a little by using gentle arm weight behind the finger. The suggested hand-crossing will keep right-hand fingers close to the chords for much of the time, thus economizing on movement. A certain depth of touch will also be needed on bass notes such as those at bars 5–7 and 25 to create an underpinning sonority. In bar 17, in the right hand, consider using fingers 4/3 and 2/1 instead of 3/2 and 3/1.

The pedal needs to be employed throughout, changing according to the harmonies, which need clarity. In places such as bars 6, 7 and 15, half-pedalling may be necessary to avoid losing the bass notes and creating textural 'holes'.

This piece can be a gate to further exploration of the gems of the French twentieth-century repertoire. A French dictionary could be useful, too!

C:3 Kadosa *Andante and Sostenuto*

These pieces will take you into the wonderful, weird world of Hungarian expression, and will appeal to pupils with a strong sense of fantasy and a lively imagination.

The Andante requires a huge range of dynamics – also subtlety within this. For example, the crescendo from bar 18 to bar 20 is enhanced if the dynamic drops slightly from the preceding *forte*, and the last two bars may benefit from a further drop to *pianissimo*. The climax, in bars 14 and 15, needs great force for which a romantically 'beautiful' tone is probably inappropriate; a certain tension in the sound will generate the necessary intensity. In the build-up to this (bars 11–14), care must be taken to observe the quaver rests. Pedalling through the grace-note flourishes then releasing a split second after the staccato quavers will guard against excessive dryness.

At the start, the printed fingering is very helpful. Smaller hands, however, might like to try dividing the grace notes, taking the lower C and G with the left hand and the upper notes with the right, using 2-4 on the Bb-D, then 1 on the second D.

The octave passage beginning in bar 18 is strongly reminiscent of a Hungarian folk instrument, the cimbalom. Try to listen to a recording of this instrument so that you can appreciate the jangling effect of this music. As this passage forms part of the climax to the piece, a slight ritardando plus an elongated 'comma' at the end can add to the drama of the moment.

The Sostenuto movement has a strong improvisatory feel, but it is a good idea to count the music precisely in the early stages of learning – rubato can only really convince if the underlying structure is understood. Thereafter, responses to the rapid changes of mood are essential: the contrast between the assertiveness of the opening gesture and the ensuing *mezzo-piano* could hardly be stronger.

Much of the rubato is already indicated in the score, but you may like to employ a split-second's delay in placing the chords in bars 6–8, to project the desired marcato effect. The dynamic range is, again, wide but there is nothing wrong in adding a few personal nuances – for example, a rise into and fall from the right-hand D in bar 16 may add interest.

Although a lot of the music will benefit from using pedal, there are places where it is less desirable. The intensity of the accents in bar 13 could be diluted by applying pedal, as could the *scorrendo* of the following bar. *Scorrendo* means gliding from note to note, and a suitable effect could be achieved by using an overlapping legato – which would be lost in continuous pedal.

Though unusual, these pieces are attractive, atmospheric additions to the repertoire. Why not explore the rest of the suite?

C:4 Bartók *Sostenuto*

For those who associate Bartók with motoric sounds, this movement and its impressionistic style will come as a surprise. The piece will certainly appeal to pupils who respond to mood and atmosphere.

Although the music does not require great dexterity, it does demand subtlety of touch, exploring semi-staccato, marcato and legato articulations. It may be a good idea to experiment with these three different touches in self-devised exercises before applying them in context. The slurred staccato chords should certainly be pedalled, probably with a change on each one, otherwise the music will sound dry and disjointed. It will sometimes be necessary to pedal through a whole bar (or more), as from bar 28 to the end. The gentle blurring caused by this is entirely within the character – just so long as the descending 10ths in the left hand are kept clean.

The proliferation of accidentals should not put the pupil off – they often disguise what are straightforward patterns. For example, the right-hand and upper left-hand sequence from bar 22 to bar 25 is composed of chromatically related major 3rds in contrary motion, and the quavers, crotchets and dotted crotchets of the last four bars employ, enharmonically, only B, E and A. You may find it helpful to redistribute the right-hand chord of bar 28, so that the B♭ and C♯ are taken by the left hand.

The melodic interest is in the upper notes of the left hand for much of the initial *Sostenuto* section (at first, doubled by the right hand's middle notes). This will need some projection, perhaps using more of the thumb tip than is normal. It may be very tempting to take the left-hand E of bars 4 and 5 with the thumb of the right hand, but be wary of losing the melodic line in the process. Note also the inner voices in bar 8.

The tempo should not be too slow, and the examiner should be able to identify an underlying pulse, despite the expressive adjustments that are called for. Your pupil will also need to practise operating within a subdued level of dynamics, since the music rarely rises much above *piano*, perhaps reaching its most intense at bar 25. Use of the *una corda* pedal could benefit the final few measures.

This piece would be a good choice for the more musically sophisticated pupil who enjoys dissonant sonorities. With its regular concurrence of major and minor within the same chord, this is a good introduction to one of Bartók's trademarks.

C:5 Sylvie Bodorová *Carousel*

Most of us love to show off with pieces that sound harder than they actually are, and here is a great addition to this type of repertoire! That said, there is plenty to get to grips with before execution becomes easy, after the relative 'whiteness' of the score has made learning the piece straightforward.

The direction at the top of the music is to go 'as fast as possible'. This may vary slightly from pupil to pupil and, while 'slow' is clearly inappropriate, one must bear in mind that *faster* than possible is not a requirement! Technically, the trickiest passage is probably bars 40–56, during which a careful sorting-out of hand positions is crucial. For example, it will be helpful to have the right-hand thumb ready for the first E in bars 41, 43 and 45 so that the following octave is already under the hand. Undisciplined fingers may well allow the tempo to run away here or become uneven, and employing a detached articulation while practising (though not in performance!) could help encourage precision. A very slight 'comma' at the end of bar 39 will prepare us for the new keyboard area, and prevent the *subito piano* being lost in the after-echo of the previous crescendo.

Careful counting in quavers, below speed, is a useful drill to ensure accuracy across the changing time signatures. This carousel (perhaps also a carousal!) does not go round in a regular manner, and much of the rhythmic effect – which is the essence in this composition – will be lost if the crotchets come out as dotted crotchets. Many varieties of articulation and texture are needed – from the dry, right-hand finger-snaps at the start to the vibrant, richly pedalled conclusion. Pedalling is clearly indicated throughout, but where the composer writes merely *con Ped.*, a suitable marcato effect may be achieved by applying direct pedal on each crotchet or dotted-crotchet chord.

The dynamics should be strongly contrasted, although it is advisable to differentiate *sforzando* within a general *piano* context (bars 2, 4 and 5) from one within a *mezzo-forte* setting (bars 24, 26 and 27). To aid the crescendo from bar 77 a slight dip in dynamic level may be appropriate, but there should be a sense of accumulation overall, climaxing in the coruscating white-note glissando, which can really attack the key bed.

All in all, this is a gift to the virtuoso temperament, and a most exhilarating concert item for both performer and listener. It also shows how accessible a piece written in 2000 can be!

C:6 Ibert *Le petit âne blanc*

This is probably Ibert's most familiar piano composition, which you may also know in its duet arrangement. The piece represents French pictorialism at its best, containing delightful trotting and 'ee-auw' effects. Though the composition may seem rather long, its A-B-A structure relies on repetition (albeit using a higher octave), thereby reducing the four pages to about two-and-a-half pages of actual learning.

A light but well-defined staccato is crucial to achieve the necessary buoyancy, especially in the left hand. Practising the scale of F sharp major in the left hand with a gentle staccato could be a useful preparatory exercise, thinking of the surface rather than the bed of the key. Adding the right hand at a very slightly louder level would then cultivate a feeling for the necessary balance between hands – without forgetting that left-hand projection is required at one point in the middle. Though the passages in double 3rds may be a new technical challenge for your pupil, a legato fingering will only be needed to connect the slurred pairs. For example, in bar 26, 5/3 to 2/1 in the right hand over 1/2 to 3/5 in the left will produce the desired effect without undue reliance on the pedal.

Observing the marked right-hand articulations is important for the eccentric onbeat/offbeat emphases of the opening (and its return). Where the instruction *Soutenu* appears, the right hand needs to feel the full depth of the key, especially with regard to the top notes, which should sing out above the rest. Take care with the accidentals in the middle section – not all that many sharps have been cancelled, and the changes need to last through the bar.

Clearly, the performance needs to be good-humoured and sparkling, with the music moving happily along but not at too fast a pace (otherwise the *tranquille* element will be lost). This allows also for a possible slight increase in speed where the composer instructs *Soudain très gai*. The dynamic level is mainly within the domain of *piano*, and even the middle episode needs some restraint if the *sforzando* 'ee-auws' are to be projected. Only once is a real *forte* required (at *En exagérant un peu les accents*) and then for less than a couple of bars. The given pedal markings, which are precise, may be helpfully extended to analogous passages, but any further usage is almost certainly unnecessary. On the other hand, application of the *una corda* will help much of the third section.

One could have much amusement imagining what might be happening in this donkey-ride. The piece has wide appeal, making it a suitable performance vehicle in a variety of contexts and leaving a smile on the face of the listener.